NOTORIOUS

At David C Cook, we equip the local church around the corner and around the globe to make disciples. Come see how we are working together—go to **www.davidccook.org**. Thank you!

NOTORIOUS

An Integrated Study
of the **ROGUES**,
SCOUNDRELS,
and **SCALLYWAGS**
of Scripture

JEFF LUCAS

DAVID **C** COOK

transforming lives together

NOTORIOUS
Published by David C Cook
4050 Lee Vance Drive
Colorado Springs, CO 80918 U.S.A.

Integrity Music Limited, a Division of David C Cook
Brighton, East Sussex BN1 2RE, England

The graphic circle C logo is a registered trademark of David C Cook.

The website addresses recommended throughout this book are offered as a
resource to you. These websites are not intended in any way to be or imply an
endorsement on the part of David C Cook, nor do we vouch for their content.

ISBN 978-0-8307-7867-6
eISBN 978-0-8307-7918-5

© 2019 Jeff Lucas

The Team: Wendi Lord, Ian Matthews, Amy Konyndyk,
Megan Stengel, Jack Campbell, Susan Murdock
Cover Design: Nick Lee
Cover Images: Getty Images

Printed in the United States of America
First Edition 2019

1 2 3 4 5 6 7 8 9 10

061519

CONTENTS

INTRODUCTION

Over the next couple of months, we are going to be looking at some of the "villains" of the Bible. We want to evaluate their fragilities and failures, see where they went wrong, and learn from their mistakes. All of them are real historical characters, with the exception of the elder brother (we read about him in the so-called parable of the prodigal son), and one of our studies will focus on a crowd rather than an individual.

In most cases, their stories ended badly, although one of the most notorious characters in our study, Saul the persecutor of the church, ultimately became Paul the great apostle, showing that our past doesn't have to define our future!

WHY ARE WE DOING THIS?

Some might argue that we would do better to study the lives of the heroes of Scripture—surely that would be more encouraging and edifying! But in inspiring Scripture, the Holy Spirit has decided to record some details of the enemies of God's purposes as well as those who followed God faithfully. Their stories are part of the overall biblical record, and so are worthy of our attention. The Bible makes it clear that there is wisdom in considering failure as well as success.

Consider what Paul said about wandering, wayward Israel: their story included seasons of idolatry, sexual immorality, testing God, and grumbling:

> For I do not want you to be ignorant of the fact, brothers and sisters, that our ancestors were all under the cloud and that they all passed through the sea. They were all baptized into Moses in the cloud and in the sea ... Nevertheless, God was not pleased with most of them; their bodies were scattered in the wilderness.
>
> Now these things occurred as examples to keep us from setting our hearts on evil things as they did ... We should not test Christ, as some of them did—and were killed by snakes. And do not grumble, as some of them did—and were killed by the destroying angel.
>
> These things happened to them as examples and were written down as warnings for us, on whom the culmination of the ages has come. (1 Cor. 10:1–2, 5–6, 9–11)

So our consideration of some of the Bible's rogues can help us as we view their examples and heed the warnings that their failures bring. Paul used the story of the wandering Hebrews as a rallying call to purity, unity, and steadfastness. And so as we look at each character, we will consider a call that his or her story amplifies.

- **Cain**—the call to authentic worship
- **The elder brother**—the call to shun graceless religion
- **Potiphar's wife**—the call to purity
- **Saul the persecutor**—the call to ongoing change and community
- **Michal, daughter of King Saul**—the call to kindness
- **Jezebel**—the call to use power and influence well
- **Judas Iscariot**—the call to surrender
- **Herod "the Great"**—the call to true greatness
- **The mob in Thessalonica**—the call to faithfulness in the war

This study will follow a simple structure for each session. As you gather in your church, community, or small groups, you will consider together what the Bible tells us about each of these characters, and have opportunity to discuss their lives, apply what you learn together, share from your own experiences, and pray together. Each session will be structured as follows:

- A question to help your group connect with one another
- Key thought for the session

- Scripture readings
- A reflection on the Bible passages
- A short video to watch together (available on the separate DVD)
- Questions for study and discussion

In addition, each session has six days of Bible notes to read and study through as part of your daily devotions, allowing the whole group to journey together during the course.

Finally, a word about villainy. We tend to categorize people—either they are good, or they are bad. In our journey, we will encounter some people who were thoroughly, consistently evil, like murderous Herod and prophet-killer Jezebel.

But most of the villains are just like us—a moral mixture capable of greatness or grime. As we ponder their stories, let's remember that they were human beings—loved of God, despite their sin—and that they are not other than us; we too can walk in the light, or go to the dark side. As we ponder them, we don't strut, arrogantly looking down on them, but rather tremble a little, lest we meander off onto our own shadowy pathways.

May God bless you as you study these rogues, scoundrels, and scallywags of Scripture!

Jeff Lucas

BIBLE STUDY TIPS

It is recommended that you make yourself familiar with each session's Scripture portion by reading it a couple of times before you meet with your group. You may want to take some notes in this book to help you prepare for the discussion with your small group.

Remember to pray as you open the Scriptures. Ask the Holy Spirit to lead you and guide you in understanding. The Bible is the inspired Word of God, so the Holy Spirit is the ultimate authority. When you are reading and interpreting meaning in the Bible, be sure to keep context in mind. A little research goes a long way. Background information and understanding the purpose of the book's main focus and the overall message of the Bible will frame a more accurate reading of the Scripture portions. It is helpful to approach the Bible as a single coherent story. Each verse, chapter, and book must be studied in light of the overall story.

A common criticism of the Bible is that you can make it say anything you wish. It goes without saying that this is a misuse of Scripture. The goal of any Bible study should be to understand God's revelation, and reading the Bible intelligently requires interpretation. The following questions will help in proper interpretation:

- What does it say?
- What did it mean to the original audience?
- How can we apply it to our lives?

Don't be intimidated if you aren't familiar with the Bible. Everyone starts somewhere, and a small group is a great place to start! If you would like to become more familiar with the Bible as a whole, a great thing to consider is reading the Bible using a reading plan of some kind. Among other places, you can access these for free online. Regular reading develops your understanding of and your appetite for the Word of God.

Enjoy the journey together!

HOW TO GET THE MOST OUT OF YOUR SMALL GROUP

SUGGESTIONS FOR A CHRIST-CENTERED SMALL GROUP

1. Invest in your growth and in your community by making a commitment to regularly and actively participate in your small group.

2. Do your part in making sure that everyone gets a chance to share in the discussion. Avoid rabbit trails!

3. Develop Christ-centered relationships with your small group members. Have an attitude of love and acceptance toward them just as Christ has for you.

4. Be respectful of everyone's journey while keeping in mind that the purpose of small groups is to seek God as He reveals Himself through His Word, the Bible.

5. Avoid cross talk, giving advice or an opinion on someone else's share. Always remember to encourage and pray for people rather than trying to fix them.

6. Be a part of your church community by being willing to ask for help when you are in need and by being willing to provide help and resources to others when they are in need.

7. Make an effort to allow yourself to be authentic and accountable.

8. Maintain healthy boundaries in life and in your relationships.

9. Have fun, and Let Love Live!

SUGGESTED ORDER

- Open with prayer.
- Read the Connecting with One Another and Key Thought sections, share the Bible reading, and work through the For Your Consideration section.
- If you are using the DVD (available separately), watch the video session.
- Continue the study and discussion.
- Use the Going Deeper section if you'd like.
- Close with prayer.

CAIN

The Call to Authentic Worship

CONNECTING WITH ONE ANOTHER

What's your favorite worship song, and why?

KEY THOUGHT THIS SESSION

We are all called to worship, and if we don't worship God His way, we'll end up worshipping something or somebody else—even ourselves!

SCRIPTURE TO READ

Genesis 4:2–16

> Now Abel kept flocks, and Cain worked the soil. In
> the course of time Cain brought some of the fruits

of the soil as an offering to the LORD. And Abel also brought an offering—fat portions from some of the firstborn of his flock. The LORD looked with favor on Abel and his offering, but on Cain and his offering he did not look with favor. So Cain was very angry, and his face was downcast.

Then the LORD said to Cain, "Why are you angry? Why is your face downcast? If you do what is right, will you not be accepted? But if you do not do what is right, sin is crouching at your door; it desires to have you, but you must rule over it."

Now Cain said to his brother Abel, "Let's go out to the field." While they were in the field, Cain attacked his brother Abel and killed him.

Then the LORD said to Cain, "Where is your brother Abel?"

"I don't know," he replied. "Am I my brother's keeper?"

The LORD said, "What have you done? Listen! Your brother's blood cries out to me from the ground. Now you are under a curse and driven from the ground, which opened its mouth to receive your brother's blood from your hand. When you work the ground, it will no longer yield its crops for you. You will be a restless wanderer on the earth."

Cain said to the LORD, "My punishment is more than I can bear. Today you are driving me from the land, and I will be hidden from your presence; I will be a restless wanderer on the earth, and whoever finds me will kill me."

But the LORD said to him, "Not so; anyone who kills Cain will suffer vengeance seven times over." Then the LORD put a mark on Cain so that no one who found him would kill him. So Cain went out from the LORD's presence and lived in the land of Nod, east of Eden.

Hebrews 11:4

By faith Abel brought God a better offering than Cain did. By faith he was commended as righteous, when God spoke well of his offerings.

1 John 3:12

Do not be like Cain, who belonged to the evil one and murdered his brother. And why did he murder him? Because his own actions were evil and his brother's were righteous.

Romans 12:1

Therefore, I urge you, brothers and sisters, in view of God's mercy, to offer your bodies as a living sacrifice, holy and pleasing to God—this is your true and proper worship.

FOR YOUR CONSIDERATION

Worship. It's a subject that can cause a lot of conversation—and conflict—among Christians. Perhaps we shouldn't be surprised at that, because the first murder recorded in human history centered on worship! Cain was envious of the divine favor that Abel enjoyed, even though both men had brought offerings of worship to the Lord.

There are many issues that arise from Cain's story, not least because the Bible makes reference to him outside of the Genesis account. It's about anger and jealousy. The writer to the Hebrews speaks of "righteous" Abel and the *faith* that he expressed in worship. Jude writes about "the way of Cain"—and most commentators think that this refers to Cain deciding to worship his way rather than God's way.

But before we consider these important lessons, let's ask: How did Cain and Abel know that one offering had been accepted, while the other was rejected? Jewish tradition has it (and Christian tradition has embraced the idea) that Abel's offering was consumed by fire that fell from heaven—that happened in five other examples in Old Testament history (Lev. 9:23–24; Judg. 6:21; 13:19–20; 1 Kings 18:30–39; 2 Chron. 7:1). Notable Christian figures like John Chrysostom, Thomas Aquinas, Martin Luther, John Owen, and Franz Delitzsch believed that fire descended on Abel's offering. Whatever the means by which approval was shown, we immediately see this principle: worship is what brings pleasure to God rather than gratifying our own personal likes and preferences. But that's not to say that there are no benefits to the worshipper.

Participating in worship can strengthen our faith, enable us to focus on what is good and true, deepen our sense of community, and grant us emotional release and strength—to name but a few of the blessings and benefits! But while worship brings us to that right place in our relationship with the Lord—He is the exalted holy One; we are His people—let's always remember that worship is primarily about ministry to God. Let's recall that truth, especially when the song or style is not to our liking!

Worship calls us to embrace mystery. We've seen that when Cain and Abel each brought their offerings, Cain's was rejected. Some commentators say that there is no explanation needed for this whatsoever, that God is God and if He chooses to disapprove for whatever reason or no reason, then that's up to Him. In a moment we'll consider some possible answers, but for now let's just affirm the truth that God does not always explain His actions, and when we try to fill in the "blanks" that we believe God has not filled, we rush into speculation and may even hurt people as a result. The most obvious example of this can be found when Christians navigate sickness.

Prayers for healing are rightly offered, but then believers start to speculate about the reasons for the sickness and possible obstacles to healing. Those who are suffering suffer more when they are told, bluntly, that they don't have enough faith, that there is sin in their lives, or that there are dark episodes in their ancestry that are causing the illness. The Bible does offer a cause-and-effect answer for some sicknesses, but to jump to conclusions and proffer a speculative "diagnosis" can be so hurtful. Let's know that it's okay not to know.

Worship also calls for *obedience*. As we've seen, some believe that when the Bible talks about "the way of Cain," this describes an attitude of wanting to worship according to how *we* want to worship, rather than in a way that God orders and prescribes. It's possible that Cain and Abel knew that worship called for a blood sacrifice (even though this obviously happened prior to the giving of the Old Testament law). In bringing an offering of an animal, perhaps Abel already saw the need for atonement for his sins. Pastor Kent Hughes wrote:

> God had evidently given explicit instructions to Cain and Abel indicating that only animal sacrifices were acceptable. Very likely they learned this through their parents, Adam and Eve, because Genesis 3:21 indicates that after that couple's sin and fall, God provided garments of animals slain to clothe their nakedness—an implicit inference that animal blood was spilled in direct response to their sin. While it is true that the categories of ritual animal sacrifices were not established until Moses' time, the earliest believers nevertheless met at the altar on the basis of blood sacrifice (Genesis 8:20–22; 15:1–11).
>
> Not only had God communicated his will regarding the necessity of animal sacrifices, but if, as we think, he communicated this first to Adam and Eve, then Cain and Abel had been conforming to the practice for some 100 years, because Cain was 129 years old at this time.[1]

Whether or not this is true, we can definitely say that worship is about sacrifice. Abel brought "portions from some of the firstborn of his flock" (Gen. 4:4)—his best. "God loves a cheerful giver" (2 Cor. 9:7), and so Abel found approval. Kent Hughes again:

> By refusing to bring the prescribed offering, and instead presenting his garden produce, he was saying that one's own good works and character is enough. Cain may have reasoned, "What I am presenting is far more beautiful than a bloody animal. I myself would prefer the lovely fruits of a harvest any day. And I worked far harder than Abel to raise my offering. It took real toil and sweat. And it is even of greater market value! Enough of this animal sacrifice business, God. My way is far better!"
>
> Cain's offering was a monument to pride and self-righteousness—"the way of Cain." Abel, on the other hand, believed and obeyed God: "By faith Abel offered God a better sacrifice than Cain did." He brought God what God wanted. This was acceptable worship.[2]

Worship calls for the right attitude as well. Abel was called "righteous," but Cain was told that sin was "crouching at the door"—perhaps offering him the chance to amend his ways. But Cain seemed determined to stay in the place of bitterness and jealousy. Perhaps he struck at his brother with an anger that he actually felt toward God; sometimes people get upset with their pastors and leaders, but the roots of their frustration are with the Lord. Since they can't directly attack God, they go for the next best available target.

When we worship God joyfully but treat each other badly, we surely nullify our worship. Love for God leads to love for others.

If you are using the DVD, watch session 1.

STUDY AND DISCUSSION

1. Why does God call us to worship? Why does He need to be praised—and does He need that?

2. Are there expressions of worship in your church that make you feel uncomfortable? Should we encourage one another to go beyond our comfort zones?

3. What does it mean to worship God sacrificially?

4. What would you say to somebody who insists that "the worship is not to their liking"? Is it okay to have a preference, and if so, when does that become a problem?

GOING DEEPER

Jealousy and anger can lead to terrible consequences. Henrik Ibsen, the playwright, said:

> I had on my table a scorpion in an empty glass.
> From time to time the brute would ail. Then I

would throw a piece of ripe fruit into it, on which it would cast itself in a rage and inject its poison into it. Then it was well again.[3]

Have you met people like this? Why does "injecting poison" into others bring relief and even joy to some?

THIS SESSION'S CHALLENGE

Jesus taught that the Father is seeking those who will worship in Spirit and truth (John 4:23–24). Ask the Lord: Am I one who worships like that? And how might I go deeper as a worshipper?

DAILY BIBLE NOTES: CAIN
Day 1. Cain: Anger

Read: Genesis 4:1–5; 1 John 3:11–24

We've witnessed it too often. The headline announces that yet another tragedy has unfolded at a school in the US, as a shooter calmly walks into a place that should be safe and takes the lives of so many innocents. While we must question the mental health of anyone who would commit such an atrocity, we realize that the root of this carnage is anger. Because of rejection, frustration, a feeling of powerlessness, anger has simmered, with terrible results.

Anger led Cain to kill his brother and become the first murderer in recorded history. As we continue to try to unravel this story of God accepting one sacrifice and rejecting another, we turn again to the New Testament to gain perspective on Cain and hear the apostle John roundly condemn him: "who belonged to the evil one and murdered his brother." John offers a motive for Cain's crime: "And why did he murder him? Because his own actions were evil and his brother's were righteous" (1 John 3:12).

Not all anger is sin. But beware lingering rage and bitterness. It usually leads to disaster.

Ponder: Has anger ever been a cause of damage in your life or in the lives of others close to you?

Day 2. Cain: Failure Is Not the End

Read: Genesis 4:1–7; Psalm 32:1

Focus: "Then the LORD said to Cain, 'Why are you angry? Why is your face downcast? If you do what is right, will you not be accepted?'" (Gen. 4:6–7).

A bright young leader was an inspiration to so many, but he hid a dark secret from nearly everybody. He battled depression that was rooted in his feeling quite shamed. After coming to Jesus as a young man, he drifted away from faith for a while, falling into some rather lurid sexual sins. For some reason, some find it more difficult to recover from failure in that area, and although he'd come back to God wholeheartedly and lived a life committed to the gospel, he couldn't pull off the shroud of shame that seemed to be draped around his soul. It didn't end well for him.

As we read John's statement that Cain "belonged to the evil one," we could be tempted to write off Cain as beyond help. But that is not what we find in the story. Encountering Cain directly, God made it clear that he had not been rejected, but that his offering had been. At this stage (before any murderous intentions surfaced), in the words that God spoke, there was a clear invitation to Cain to do right and thus know approval—another opportunity for another day. Sadly, anger, and perhaps shame, won the day, and Cain continued his downhill trek into tragedy and judgment, and Abel lost his life.

We all fail, but some of us view failure as a terminal act, which is quite wrong. If you've fallen, get up and allow grace to turn your downcast face into a smile of relief and joy once more. There is hope and help for a better day ahead as we celebrate the joy of being forgiven.

Pray: Help me to accept the gift of grace that You offer, Lord—the gift that brings hope when I feel hopeless about myself. Amen.

Day 3. Cain: Sin Crouches

Read: Genesis 4:1–7; Romans 6:12–14

Focus: "But if you do not do what is right, sin is crouching at your door; it desires to have you, but you must rule over it" (Gen. 4:7).

During a day out in the high country in the Colorado mountains, we suddenly stumbled upon a rather large moose grazing beneath a nearby tree. These huge animals are infamous for being tetchy;

irritate them at your peril, because they have been known to charge passing trains, which is not a sign of great intelligence. We edged closer, bold because of the nonchalant attitude of the moose, who didn't appear to be aware of his visitors. But he was fooling us. In a moment, his head came up, and he broke into a charge. He had us in his sights. We felt led to get out of his way! Thankfully, though, he ran out of steam before he could reach us. Still, it was quite a worrying moment.

As God spoke to Cain about sin, He painted a picture of a crouching animal that, as one translator put it, "is eager to be at you." This speaks of the deceptive, compulsive power of sin and temptation, promising much, urging us to surrender to its wiles, subtle in its attack. No wonder we need to be aware of our weaknesses and diligent about our choices. But there's hope from God even in the warning to Cain, because he is told to master his sinful inclinations. The call to mastery obviously shows that Cain was not a helpless victim of temptation, but that he could have conquered it.

Sometimes we excuse our behavior, insisting that we "just can't help it." We're only human, we insist. But that's not true. With the help of God's Spirit, we can rule over that which seeks to rule over us. Sin crouches. Tackle it, with God's help.

Pray: Today I will be vigilant, Father, aware of temptation, yet not intimidated by it. Amen.

Day 4. Premeditated and Consistent Sin

Read: Genesis 4:1–16; Jude verse 11

Focus: "While they were in the field, Cain attacked his brother Abel and killed him" (Gen. 4:8).

Murder is obviously always horrifying, but the specific details of the first murder in history are especially chilling, not least because this was a brother killing his own brother, his own flesh and blood. And although we've already seen that Cain was driven by anger, this was not a sudden impetuous act, a crime of passion. Cain was guilty of a premeditated, deliberate crime that involved careful planning. Luring Abel with an invitation to a walk in the fields, Cain killed him in cold blood. Questioned by God as to the whereabouts of his brother (God knew but asked the question anyway, perhaps to further test Cain's integrity, or lack of it), Cain lied to the Lord and feigned ignorance of his brother's location.

So why all this sin upon sin? Commenting on this terrible episode, theologian Dietrich Bonhoeffer suggested that hatred for God was the root of Cain's violence and rage. It was God who rejected Cain's sacrifice, and it was God who ultimately created Abel, whom Cain viewed as a rival rather than a brother. But while God is obviously impervious to violent actions against Him, other humans are vulnerable. As a Christian leader, I've seen this principle at work: when people are enraged at God, they will lash out at those whom they see as representatives of Him, such as their local minister or pastor. Bitterness multiples sin—and hurts those who don't deserve our ire. Are you engaged in a battle with someone whom you're using to vent your frustration?

Pray: Lord, when I'm struggling in my relationship with You, save me from taking out that frustration on others. Amen.

Day 5. The Hero: "Righteous" Abel

Read: Matthew 23:13–36; 1 Peter 4:12–19

Focus: "And so upon you will come all the righteous blood that has been shed on earth, from the blood of righteous Abel to the blood of Zechariah son of Berekiah, whom you murdered between the temple and the altar" (Matt. 23:35).

It's a lingering myth that we all want to believe: the idea that those who walk with God will not suffer. If that idea seems far-fetched, remember that there are still bestselling authors and television evangelists who hawk the idea that we can avoid bumps in the road of life if we have enough faith. Not only is much of this teaching "faith in faith," but it is also totally misleading. In confronting the rank hypocrisy of the self-righteous Pharisees, Jesus called Abel "righteous"—the ultimate accolade! And as we've already seen, Abel appears in the "Hebrews hall of faith." So far from lacking faith, he is celebrated as one of the greatest faith heroes in human history. And yet still he died at the hands of his murderous brother. Not only was he unprotected, but his righteousness was the reason for his demise.

Anyone who suggests that faith is a sure guarantee of an easy life only needs to look at the example of the twelve disciples. With the obvious exception of Judas (and the apostle John, who was exiled in Patmos), all died martyrs' deaths.

Around the world today, good and faithful followers of Jesus are suffering for their faith. They could live untroubled lives if they would just abandon their commitment to Christ, but despite their suffering, they stand firm. Remember to pray for them, their families, and for the authorities that oppress them today. And if you're suffering today, especially because of your faith, I'm praying that you'll be strengthened—but not surprised.

Pray: Grant strength and hope to those who suffer for Your name's sake, Father. And grant revelation and repentance to those who oppress Your people. Amen.

Day 6. Living Worship

Read: Hebrews 11:1–4; John 4:1–26

Focus: "By faith Abel brought God a better offering than Cain did. By faith he was commended as righteous, when God spoke well of his offerings. And by faith Abel still speaks, even though he is dead" (Heb. 11:4).

If you've been a Christian for any amount of time, you've probably sung a lot of songs and attended a lot of worship services! There's a danger that worship can become a dull routine, a lifeless weekend ritual. Before we move on from Cain's sad story, we should consider one other theory about why his offering was rejected. Some commentators believe that Abel brought a living thing for sacrifice and that worship should be living and vibrant, not coldly mechanical. That doesn't mean that we will always *feel* like worshipping, or that excitement about faith should be the constant norm for all Christians. We worship, not because of what we feel, but because of who God is!

Our worship should always be an act of faith. We've already seen that the writer to the Hebrews celebrated Abel's faith. When we worship, we speak, sing, and bring praise to One whom we cannot see. Perhaps we worship from a place of confusion and struggle. Our worship then is truly an act of faith, not the result of certain feelings, which come and go. Ultimately our worship is a response to the call of the Father, who "seeks" those who will worship authentically—and that includes our gatherings of prayer, praise, and teaching, as well as the way we live our everyday lives.

Pray: Let my life, my prayers, my song be true acts of worship in Your sight, loving Father. Amen.

THE ELDER BROTHER

The Call to Shun Graceless Religion

CONNECTING WITH ONE ANOTHER

What was the best party you've ever attended? What made it so memorable?

KEY THOUGHT THIS SESSION

Religious people can become intolerant, ungracious, and condemning. We all need to beware the "virus" or "yeast" of Pharisaism.

SCRIPTURE TO READ

Luke 15:1–2

> Now the tax collectors and sinners were all gathering around to hear Jesus. But the Pharisees and the

teachers of the law muttered, "This man welcomes sinners and eats with them."

Luke 15:11–32

Jesus continued: "There was a man who had two sons. The younger one said to his father, 'Father, give me my share of the estate.' So he divided his property between them.

"Not long after that, the younger son got together all he had, set off for a distant country and there squandered his wealth in wild living. After he had spent everything, there was a severe famine in that whole country, and he began to be in need. So he went and hired himself out to a citizen of that country, who sent him to his fields to feed pigs. He longed to fill his stomach with the pods that the pigs were eating, but no one gave him anything.

"When he came to his senses, he said, 'How many of my father's hired servants have food to spare, and here I am starving to death! I will set out and go back to my father and say to him: Father, I have sinned against heaven and against you. I am no longer worthy to be called your son; make me like one of your hired servants.' So he got up and went to his father.

"But while he was still a long way off, his father saw him and was filled with compassion for him;

he ran to his son, threw his arms around him and kissed him.

"The son said to him, 'Father, I have sinned against heaven and against you. I am no longer worthy to be called your son.'

"But the father said to his servants, 'Quick! Bring the best robe and put it on him. Put a ring on his finger and sandals on his feet. Bring the fattened calf and kill it. Let's have a feast and celebrate. For this son of mine was dead and is alive again; he was lost and is found.' So they began to celebrate.

"Meanwhile, the older son was in the field. When he came near the house, he heard music and dancing. So he called one of the servants and asked him what was going on. 'Your brother has come,' he replied, 'and your father has killed the fattened calf because he has him back safe and sound.'

"The older brother became angry and refused to go in. So his father went out and pleaded with him. But he answered his father, 'Look! All these years I've been slaving for you and never disobeyed your orders. Yet you never gave me even a young goat so I could celebrate with my friends. But when this son of yours who has squandered your property with prostitutes comes home, you kill the fattened calf for him!'

"'My son,' the father said, 'you are always with me, and everything I have is yours. But we had to celebrate and be glad, because this brother of

yours was dead and is alive again; he was lost and
is found.'"

Matthew 16:6

In the meantime, Jesus said to them, "Keep a sharp
eye out for Pharisee-Sadducee yeast." (THE MESSAGE)

FOR YOUR CONSIDERATION

It's a familiar but effective technique in storytelling. As the tale unfolds,
the obvious villain turns out to be a good guy, and the one we thought
was trustworthy is actually the snake in the grass. Jesus used that technique in the story we commonly know as the parable of the prodigal
son. He painted a shocking word portrait of the young son, crafted to
be especially offensive to Jewish sensibilities. The lad treats his father as
if he is already dead in demanding his share of the inheritance and then
stomps off to a life of waste and squalor, ultimately ending up in the
company of some very nonkosher pigs. Even his decision to head back
home is flawed and selfish, driven by a rumbling stomach rather than a
pricked conscience. Surely he is the rascal of the story.

But there's a sudden twist as the elder brother heads for home at
the end of another hard day's work on the farm. The elder brother
turns out to be the true rebel, the rogue of the piece.

Remember, this is a fictional story that Jesus told, a parable rather
than a historical episode. But we can learn from the elder brother's
villainy. And the first lesson is this: we can end up being bad while all
the time thinking we're doing good.

Jesus' story was pointed: He told this parable in direct response to muttered criticism from some Pharisees. Jesus used specific wording in His storytelling to make it clear who He was addressing—the "elder" brother was *presbuteros*, a word used to describe the elders of the people, especially the scribes, who were partners in critical crime with the Pharisees. Fastidious in their religiosity, they had become just like the elder brother in this story. For them, religion had gone wrong.

When faith makes us feel superior, when we become picky and critical, and when we refuse to pass grace around, we become the villains of the story. But like the elder brother, sometimes we are quite unaware that we're doing wrong. We don't know what we don't know.

The two brothers in this parable are the subject of a well-known Arabic phrase, "Each one of them is worse than the other." How apt that Eastern logic applies to these two boys. The parable uses the imagery of distance poignantly—both sons start from the place of being outside. Both try to act like servants. The younger wants to work off his debt, and the elder, while all along a son, has lived like a slave for years, at least in his head and heart. Both demand payment in the story—either his share of the inheritance, or a goat for a private party. Each one wants something from the father to satisfy his own interests. Each insults his father, although the elder brother's insult is greater, an episode of public shaming. Manipulation is attempted by both of them, and each one moves toward a community away from the father and the father's friends: the prodigal, in the far country, and the elder brother, his pals with whom he wants to share a barbecue. To each, the Father shows his costly, sacrificial, patient love, even as they threaten the unity of the entire family by their selfishness. Both are prodigals.

Passionate Christians Can Turn into Older Brothers

For the prudent, the faithful, the zealous, the subtle temptation of religious slavery awaits, a well-camouflaged trap that has snapped over the heels of too many. Driven by our false notions of what God is like, not only do some of us work ourselves into the ground, but we labor joylessly because we're sullenly convinced that God can never quite be appeased.

Some believe God has a default mechanism—that He is angry and He needs to be persuaded to love. Their God is a heartless despot. So it is that those with a view of God like this will spend many years—tragically in some cases, a lifetime—frantically doing things for God. And the deeper tragedy is this: God never asked them to do most of those things in the first place. He isn't looking for slaves, only adopted sons and daughters.

When the prodigal returns home and presents his entirely logical plan to join his father's workforce, his dad will have none of it. It was simply unacceptable to the father to have one of his sons as a slave. But the elder brother, having worked for years with the heart and mind of a slave, blames his father for his condition. And he goes on to blatantly malign his father too, complaining that he's never been given even a young goat, whereas, in fact, he's been handed the title deeds to two-thirds of the entire farm.

The elder brother lived beneath his privileges for too long. When we live less than an abundant Christian life, the whole thing becomes a tedious trudge, and we become angry at God, and resentful of anyone who is living a more exciting and fulfilled Christian experience than we are—like the returning prodigal, for example. And now resentment has seeped into his heart; not only is he incensed with his kid brother, but he is irate with his father too, just as the Pharisees were angry and critical of Jesus. Perhaps we've realized that we've lost a lot of our lives fretting about things that God never asked us to concern ourselves with. We were badly taught, and we unthinkingly downloaded demands that came from zealous humans, and not from the heart of God.

Near Eastern commentators have noticed that the elder brother never uses the common greeting "O father," as respect and intimacy would demand in that culture. He just launches into an abusive tirade. "Elder brothers" are often faithful in church, conscientious givers, and morally scrupulous and doctrinally orthodox. But some lose their astonishment about being forgiven; the spiritual honeymoon is long over, and now they live in a worn-out marriage to God, where there is no intimacy or spontaneity, and very little conversation. The marriage continues, but more because of fear and duty. The wonderful father figure first offers himself to his young son. Now, he himself goes out to plead with his oldest boy (rather than hastily dispatching a servant with an order to sort the troublemaker out, whatever it took). And if our hearts have become cold, indifferent, and unmoved, and so we have become prodigals in the pew, then God offers Himself afresh to us too.

One of the tragic characteristics of the elder brother is that he wants to exclude. The Pharisees did the same, incensed that Jesus was having table fellowship with "sinners." But God calls us to radical inclusivity and welcome.

The level of self-deception that lurks in the heart of big brother is frightening. He is blatantly disobeying his father, who has come personally to escort him into the banquet. His out-of-control tirade is beyond belief in a culture where to publicly dishonor someone was a terrible crime, hence the rabbinic saying: "It is better for a man that he should cast himself into a fiery furnace rather than that he should put his fellow to shame in public."

The big brother shames not just anyone, but his own father. Near Eastern listeners would expect a strong reaction from the father in the story—servants would be sent, and the brother would perhaps be beaten for his dishonorable, scandalous behavior. One ancient commentator wrote:

> In his refusal to enter, the older son demonstrated maliciousness of character and meanness. He has no love for his brother and no appropriate respect for his father.[1]

And yet even as he commits such a blatant, hurtful crime, he protests his own innocence and faithfulness: "I never disobeyed your orders."

He looks back over the years and sees only unbroken obedience, but even as he speaks, he stands in the place of total rebellion. Elder brothers fail to see their pride, arrogance, judgmentalism, and their own need for grace. No wonder Jesus warned us not to become like those infamous rogues of the New Testament, the Pharisees, who personified the "spirit" of the elder brother.

Passion doesn't make us right. On the surface, the Pharisees looked like piously dedicated souls, guardians of orthodoxy. The Jewish historian Philo, a contemporary of Jesus and Paul, described them as "full of zeal for the laws, the strictest guardians of the ancestral traditions."

The Pharisees believed that it was more valuable to study the law than engage in temple worship. They wanted to end all divisions between the sacred and the secular, and rightly taught that the whole of life should be lived before God (and this ironically was part of their downfall; their desire to see every meal as an act of worship meant that they were unable to share meals with "sinners," which bought them into direct conflict with Jesus). Far from being dead traditionalists, they were passionate reformers, insisting that God's presence was not limited to a special building, but, as it said in the Mishnah, "if two sit together and study Torah, the Divine Presence rests between them."

When we first meet the elder brother, we hear that he has been working in the field: hardworking (even working late!) and conscientious. He's passionate about the farm.

The Pharisees prayed for three hours a day, longed for a revival in Israel, and had high hopes for a messianic figure who would come to rescue the nation.

Again, passion is no sign that we're right. Ironically, passionate people are often the ones who cause trouble in churches. They have little time for those who don't measure up to their standards, and their passion sometimes fuels conflict. Let's be passionate about our faith—but beware the power of misguided passion.

If you are using the DVD, watch session 2.

STUDY AND DISCUSSION

1. What kind of attitudes should we embrace to avoid the "yeast" of Pharisaism?

2. The elder brother was blind to his own rebellion. Judgmental people are often not aware of their own frailties and sins because they focus on the "speck" in other people's eyes rather than the "log" in their own. How can we avoid this blindness?

3. Why do some Christians act like slaves rather than sons and daughters of God?

4. What are the influences that shape our view of what God is like? Have you had some negative views of God that have been changed as you've traveled the journey of faith?

GOING DEEPER

Theologian Catherine Mowry LaCugna described the call for us to welcome and be inclusive:

> Living the Trinitarian faith means living as Jesus Christ lived; preaching the gospel; relying totally upon God; offering healing and reconciliation; rejecting laws, customs and conventions that place people beneath rules; resisting temptation; praying constantly; eating with modern day lepers and other outcasts; embracing the enemy and the sinner; dying for the sake of the gospel if it is God's will.[2]

How might that look in our context today?

THIS SESSION'S CHALLENGE

Ask the Holy Spirit to show you any areas of your life where you have become proud, arrogant, or judgmental. And ask Him to give you a fresh revelation of the fatherhood of God in your life.

DAILY BIBLE NOTES: THE ELDER BROTHER
Day 1. The Elder Brother

Read: Luke 15:11–32; Matthew 23:1–12

It's one of the most misnamed stories of the Bible: the parable of the prodigal son. It *is* about a wayward boy who finds amazing grace. It *is* about a father who sprints down the road to welcome him home. But there's a sense in which the key figure in the story is the elder brother, who represents religion gone very wrong.

As Jesus told the story, it seemed there was going to be one of those "and they all lived happily ever after" endings. But it wasn't to be. The prodigal, so recently very far away, is restored now, safe in the house, reconciled to his father, thrilled by the party, if not somewhat concerned about the fracas taking place outside. But his elder brother has taken his place and become the new prodigal. He is outside, and for the second time that day, the father has to go out to a wayward son. But this one shows no signs of wanting to join the party.

One Near Eastern scholar offered this translation describing the moment the father tried to reason with his eldest son: "His father came out searching for him." It's the same word used to describe the shepherd who lost a sheep, and the woman who lost a coin, earlier in Luke. Suddenly the gang of muttering Pharisees, listening intently to every word that Jesus spoke, were confronted with a mirror image of themselves. Big brother was outside the house and intent on staying there. They, often known as the elders as we mentioned, realize that he represents them. Jesus was telling them that they were prodigals too. This is a story that features the prodigal sons. There were definitely two. Sadly, only one of them realized it. This shows us an important truth: religion can be bad for you!

Jesus taught His disciples to "beware the leaven" of the Pharisees and Sadducees. We can all be vulnerable. Be passionate for Jesus, but not pharisaic.

Ponder: Why do passionate Christians sometimes turn into pharisaic Christians?

Day 2. "Elder Brothers" Don't Like Parties

Read: Luke 15:25–27, 31–32

Focus: "When he came near the house, he heard music and dancing. So he called one of the servants and asked him what was going on" (Luke 15:25–26).

The man was angry, his nostrils wide, and I'm pretty sure I actually heard a snort. "This doesn't seem like a Christian event to me," he said, eyes narrowing. "These young people are having … having way too much … fun!" The word "fun" came out like an expletive, as if fun was the last thing that any committed follower of Jesus should be having. I glanced over at the stage, where a gaggle of young people were bopping around, enjoying the end of a rather frantic day of seminars and Bible studies. But the fact that they were having such a good time was offensive to the snorting critic.

Jesus painted a picture of a full-on Jewish party—the elder brother *heard* the sound of music and dancing before he saw anyone. And it was quite a feast—a fattened calf would normally only be killed for a minimum of two hundred guests. In the Old Testament, the killing of a calf was only for very special occasions. It was seen as a meal fit for angels: Abraham was visited by three angels (Gen. 18) and he offered them a calf. It was also a feast fit for royalty: King Saul and his servants had a calf butchered for them (1 Sam. 28).

Laughter, shared meals, and good, clean fun—these should surely be part of the life of any healthy church community.

If we are nervous or condemning of good fun, we should ask ourselves the question, why?

Pray: May I be a carrier of joy as a follower of Yours, Father. Amen.

Day 3. "Elder Brothers" Are Angry and Stubborn

Read: Luke 15:25–29; Proverbs 18:19

Focus: "So he called one of the servants and asked him what was going on. 'Your brother has come,' he replied, 'and your father has killed the fattened calf because he has him back safe and sound.' The older brother became angry and refused to go in" (Luke 15:26–28).

Some people live angry. Even on days when things are going their way, they seem to be parked on the edge of anger all the time, and people close to them tread carefully, knowing that they could explode at any time. And anger and stubbornness often go hand in hand. Angry people easily become entrenched in their own opinions and refuse to budge, even when it becomes apparent that they are quite wrong. They will not be moved. Proverbs paints a stark picture of the offended person who refuses to shift in their position of anger.

In the parable, the father figure does everything he can to persuade his irate son to join the party. There's an interesting contrast in the wording that we can easily miss because we read the story in English. When the elder brother summons the servant and demands to know the reason for the spontaneous party, the word used means "to stand in front of"—a posture of interrogation. But when Jesus described the interaction between the father and the elder brother, the word changes and means "to come alongside." The word used is rooted in the term *paraclete*, which is a biblical name for the Holy Spirit, who comes alongside to comfort and help us.

If you're involved in a standoff right now, in a conflict where neither party is blinking and nobody is willing to give way, realize that as you stand with your feet planted and your arms folded, God might be pleading with you to act differently. Who knows? Perhaps there's a celebration ahead.

Pray: Life—and people—can be frustrating, Lord. When anger fills me, and I am tempted to become entrenched, show me the way. Amen.

Day 4. The Elder Brother: You're Not Welcome Here

Read: Luke 15:28–30; 2 Corinthians 5:18

Focus: "But when this son of yours who has squandered your property with prostitutes comes home, you kill the fattened calf for him!" (Luke 15:30).

One of the characteristics of "elder brother" syndrome is a failure to welcome people who don't look and sound like us. Religion makes us exclusive; instead of being welcoming, we become people who are "holier than thou."

When Jesus talked about an oldest brother who refused to participate in a community feast, His hearers would have been very shocked, because there was a cultural expectation that the elder brother would act as host at any family gathering. Those who first heard the story would have expected it to play out something like this:

"There was a man who had two sons. The younger one said to his father, 'Father, give me my share of the estate.' The older son, knowing that it was his responsibility to intervene and mediate in this developing conflict, came between his younger brother and his beloved father and did everything in his power to reconcile them. A peace was brokered. They all lived happily ever after. And great was the relief of the fattened calf."

In a family dispute like this, it would always be the responsibility of the oldest son in the family to step in. So according to the culture of the day, the elder brother here failed on two fronts: as a host and as a mediator.

Even if he hated his brother, he would still fulfill this task for the sake of his father, but here the older son refuses.

People around us need to be reconciled to God and welcomed into God's family. Let's all play our part.

Pray: Lord, may my life cause others to want to come home to You; may my welcome warm their hearts when they come. Amen.

Day 5. "Elder Brothers" Live Like Resentful Slaves

Read: Luke 15:28–29; John 15:1–17

Focus: "So his father went out and pleaded with him. But he answered his father, 'Look! All these years I've been slaving for you'" (Luke 15:28–29).

Here's a blunt statement I'd like you to ponder: as Christians, we can either live like slaves or live like sons and daughters of God. Over the years, I've met thousands of Christians, and I've encountered far too many who live fearful, cringing lives, never quite at peace, never fully confident that the Lord absolutely loves them as they are. Often these people are the ones who work so very hard as volunteers in the local church and beyond: they are pillars, and nobody can doubt their hard work—but tragically they are driven by an endless need to do more. Instead of being motivated by the wonderful, secure love of God, they are rather compelled to work harder, always trying to gain God's approval, never settled in the truth that He already utterly loves and approves of them.

That kind of drivenness ultimately leads to resentment. The elder brother's angry outburst shows that he resents his father and has even been reluctant to ask him for blessing: "I never once asked for a young goat so that I could celebrate with my friends ..."

But it can also lead to self-deception, because the elder brother protests that he has never once disobeyed his father's orders, even while he stubbornly refuses to join the party, resolutely refusing to obey his father's order! Contrast that with the returning prodigal, who is inside the house, wearing new shoes—only family members could wear shoes in the house; servants had to go barefoot. Be at peace. You're home safe.

Pray: Having become Your child, may I never act like a driven servant, Father. May my heart be at rest in Your love. Amen.

Day 6. The Elder Brother: Write Your Own Ending

Read: Luke 15:1–32; Proverbs 3:5–6

Perhaps it's happened to you too. You're watching a movie, totally engrossed in the story, when it comes to a sudden end, without the loose ends of the plot being tied up. You're left, not with a conclusion, but with a question mark. What happened to the villain? Did that couple live happily ever after? You're left hanging; your questions unanswered. It's gutting.

And now there are even some movies available where you can choose your own ending. Some director's cut films offer deleted scenes where you can conclude the story in a number of different ways. What will happen to that villain, that couple? You decide. Press here for ending A.

As Jesus concluded His prodigal son story, we are left wondering what happened. The elder brother is still outside the house, his father pleading with him. The returned prodigal is still in the house, enjoying the party, the community gathered to celebrate.

But we're left standing on tiptoe. What happened next? Did the elder brother ever see the error of his stubbornness and go into the party and begin greeting the guests? Were the two brothers reconciled? Was there a happy ending?

We never find out. Perhaps Jesus did this deliberately, to allow the Pharisees—and us—to construct their own endings.

Perhaps you are at a critical junction in your own personal story at the moment. The decision that you are about to make could set your course for a very, very long time. Pause, pray, think, and then repeat. And may you choose wisely and well.

Pray: When I come to the crossroad moments in life, guide me, mighty God, that I might walk in Your ways and do Your will. Amen.

POTIPHAR'S WIFE

The Call to Purity

CONNECTING WITH ONE ANOTHER

Think of two unusual facts about yourself that you can share with the rest of the group: one that is true, and make the other one up! After each person shares, have the group vote on which one is true.

KEY THOUGHT THIS SESSION

The story we consider this session is not just about sexual immorality and temptation; it's also about disloyalty and lies. One character flaw can lead to many others.

SCRIPTURE TO READ

Genesis 39:1–23

Now Joseph had been taken down to Egypt. Potiphar, an Egyptian who was one of Pharaoh's officials, the captain of the guard, bought him from the Ishmaelites who had taken him there.

The LORD was with Joseph so that he prospered, and he lived in the house of his Egyptian master. When his master saw that the LORD was with him and that the LORD gave him success in everything he did, Joseph found favor in his eyes and became his attendant. Potiphar put him in charge of his household, and he entrusted to his care everything he owned. From the time he put him in charge of his household and of all that he owned, the LORD blessed the household of the Egyptian because of Joseph. The blessing of the LORD was on everything Potiphar had, both in the house and in the field. So Potiphar left everything he had in Joseph's care; with Joseph in charge, he did not concern himself with anything except the food he ate.

Now Joseph was well-built and handsome, and after a while his master's wife took notice of Joseph and said, "Come to bed with me!"

But he refused. "With me in charge," he told her, "my master does not concern himself with anything in the house; everything he owns he has entrusted to my care. No one is greater in this house than I am. My master has withheld nothing from me except you, because you are his wife. How then could I do such a wicked thing and sin against God?" And though she spoke to Joseph day after day, he refused to go to bed with her or even be with her.

One day he went into the house to attend to his duties, and none of the household servants was inside. She caught him by his cloak and said, "Come to bed with me!" But he left his cloak in her hand and ran out of the house.

When she saw that he had left his cloak in her hand and had run out of the house, she called her household servants. "Look," she said to them, "this Hebrew has been brought to us to make sport of us! He came in here to sleep with me, but I screamed. When he heard me scream for help, he left his cloak beside me and ran out of the house."

She kept his cloak beside her until his master came home. Then she told him this story: "That Hebrew slave you brought us came to me to make sport of me. But as soon as I screamed for help, he left his cloak beside me and ran out of the house."

When his master heard the story his wife told him, saying, "This is how your slave treated me," he burned with anger. Joseph's master took him and put him in prison, the place where the king's prisoners were confined.

But while Joseph was there in the prison, the LORD was with him; he showed him kindness and granted him favor in the eyes of the prison warden. So the warden put Joseph in charge of all those held in the prison, and he was made responsible for all that was done there. The warden paid no attention to anything under Joseph's care, because the LORD was with Joseph and gave him success in whatever he did.

Psalm 119:69–70

> Though the arrogant have smeared me with lies,
>> I keep your precepts with all my heart.
> Their hearts are callous and unfeeling,
>> but I delight in your law.

FOR YOUR CONSIDERATION

Sexual temptation is everywhere. Pornography is easily available on the internet, and the statistics about Christians who use online porn are far from encouraging. What used to be seen as "soft" pornography now regularly appears in mainstream movies and television series. Casual encounters can be easily arranged, again online. And the church is an ideal place for immorality to rear its ugly head: we build close relationships, often sharing our lives with a measure of intimacy. We affirm our love for one another, and hugs are commonplace: close community is an ideal place for lines to be crossed.

In recent years there have been a series of ugly news stories about high-profile businesspeople, entertainers, and power players who have allegedly used their positions to oppress, abuse, and molest. And the church scene has not been without its scandals either. Whether it be heartbreaking stories of priests abusing little children or popular evangelical personalities engaging in inappropriate behavior, our hearts ache for the victims. Thank God that they are finally finding the courage to tell their stories.

These scandals underline the need for us all to be diligent—Scripture calls us to absolute sexual purity. The apostle Paul called the believers in Rome to live "in the light":

> Let us behave decently, as in the daytime, not in carousing and drunkenness, not in sexual immorality and debauchery, not in dissension and jealousy. (Rom. 13:13)

And he wrote to the Ephesians, calling them to shun not only sexual impurity but greed too:

> But among you there must not be even a hint of sexual immorality, or of any kind of impurity, or of greed, because these are improper for God's holy people. (Eph. 5:3)

The story of Potiphar's wife is a revealing saga about sexual temptation. But it's also about false accusation. While we should be glad that victims are speaking out, some caution is needed too. In the atmosphere of outrage that exists, justice can become a casualty, as people are removed from positions without the opportunity to defend themselves, and before any convincing proof is shown. An accusation seems enough to convict and sentence these days, with the jury of the press and public opinion rushing to judgment. Let's continue to pray that victims will have the courage to speak out, and find peace and well-deserved justice. And let's also pray that there will be no new victims because of false accusation, their lives smeared and their careers damaged because of lies. All victimization is wrong.

Thirty-five hundred years ago, Joseph became a victim, and all because of a woman called … well, her name isn't ever mentioned in the biblical story; she is simply known as Potiphar's wife.

She was relentless, and kept on urging Joseph to sin. Temptation is a daily reality, and it's persistent. Joseph was an ideal target, because like his beautiful mother Rachel, he was very good looking (Gen. 29:17)—a blessing that can easily become a curse. He had also experienced an amazing promotion to power, which could have gone to his head. Success makes some feel that they don't need to abide by the rules that everyone else follows—they are special, at least in their own eyes. And then Joseph was young, probably just seventeen or eighteen years old at the time, and so his hormones would have been racing (Gen. 37:2). Nobody would ever know; Joseph was alone with the lady of the house.

Potiphar's wife wouldn't take no for an answer. Having first made a bold proposal ("Let's go to bed"—nothing subtle about that approach), she kept trying to wear Joseph down, day after day. The language of the text implies that she even softened her advances, asking him to just spend a little time with her. But then her final approach was really an assault. We read that she grabbed Joseph by the cloak, but that's a genteel way of putting it. Some commentators suggest that she grabbed his undergarment.

But in the face of this continued onslaught, Joseph remained true to his convictions, and resisted, even though his good choices would ultimately lead to further trouble.

Joseph had known deprivation and rejection, himself a victim of human trafficking because of his brothers' treachery. But here he found himself in a place of blessing and responsibility, selected by one of Pharaoh's senior officials, a captain of the guard, to be the man in charge of his household. In this story we repeatedly hear that God was the source of the blessing that rested upon Joseph. But being in the place of blessing, in the very center of God's will, did not remove the possibility of temptation from the young man. Diligence is always needed.

But we don't stand alone when temptation comes—help is at hand. Although Joseph made good choices (in stark contrast to Potiphar's wife, who consistently made ugly decisions driven by lust, betrayal, and false accusation), God was the source not only of Joseph's success, but of his resilience too.

When we dig into the text, we discover that in this episode the God who was "with" Joseph is referred to no fewer than eight times by His covenant name (Yahweh). It doesn't happen again in the remaining account of Joseph (all eight chapters of it), except when Jacob used that name of God as he died (Gen. 49:18). Scripture wants to make it clear that persistence is the greatest threat of temptation, and that God is with us and can strengthen us for the fight of faith.

> No test or temptation that comes your way is
> beyond the course of what others have had to face.
> All you need to remember is that God will never

let you down; he'll never let you be pushed past your limit; he'll always be there to help you come through it. (1 Cor. 10:13 THE MESSAGE)

Fight the good fight of the faith. (1 Tim. 6:12)

We can be especially susceptible to temptation when we feel low, or betrayed. Joseph could have excused himself with some rationalization: "Life's treated me harshly, so a little comfort is reasonable enough ..."

> Joseph knew the dysfunction of a father's favoritism (37:3), the scorn of ten brothers' hatred (37:4–5, 8), the betrayal of being sold for profit by those responsible for him (37:27–28), the disdain of a slave's life as chattel (37:36; 39:1), and the dissolution of transplantation to foreign soil and culture (39:1). With this as his bio, Joseph had every reason to be angry, bitter, resentful, cynical, fearful, self-serving, and self-pitying.... Joseph had every human reason to find fleeting solace in an illicit embrace.[1]

The scheming of Potiphar's wife also demonstrates a truth that we sometimes find hard to hear: doing the right thing is no guarantee that we will be spared trial.

Even though God would ultimately promote Joseph in prison, that didn't make being incarcerated an easy thing to endure.

Historians tell us that conditions were terrible in Egyptian prisons thirty-five hundred years ago.

Life is often unfair, and will include times of temptation when our character will be tested. God never promises that we will *escape* trouble, but He does assure us that we will never be abandoned by Him *in* trouble.

Joseph's life shines brilliantly when compared to the murky character of Potiphar's wife—her story is about self-preoccupation and sin. Joseph, however, is a picture of true success, not just promotion and power, but character development too. Though he was certainly not an overnight success; even his promotion in Potiphar's house was gradual. First, he was promoted to work indoors, instead of being an agricultural slave. Then, having "pleased his master," he became his personal attendant, finally being the senior staffer in the household, trusted with all that his employer-master had. Success calls for hard work and endurance—even when God is with you.

If you are using the DVD, watch session 3.

STUDY AND DISCUSSION

1. How can we be healthily diligent in our relationships without becoming paranoid?

2. What are some of the devastating results of immorality?

3. If you were asked to speak on the topic of "true success" to a group of graduating high school students, what might your message be?

GOING DEEPER

We've affirmed the truth that God wants to help us when we are tempted, but how does He do that exactly?

THIS SESSION'S CHALLENGE

Potiphar's wife showed no restraint, no desire to operate according to any moral compass, while Joseph ran from temptation. Are there any areas in our lives where we are courting temptation, convincing ourselves that we can escape it at any time, but unwittingly becoming increasingly ensnared?

DAILY BIBLE NOTES: POTIPHAR'S WIFE
Day 1. Potiphar's Wife: Betraying Trust

Read: Genesis 39:1–8; Ecclesiastes 5:4–8

Focus: "But he refused. 'With me in charge,' he told her, 'my master does not concern himself with anything in the house; everything he owns he has entrusted to my care'" (Gen. 39:8).

Okay, so it happened forty years ago now, but the day still lingers in my memory as one of the most special. It was our wedding day. We had very little materially, virtually no spending money for our honeymoon, and were secretly hoping that some of our wedding guests might give us cash as gifts rather than the obligatory toaster. That day we exchanged promises, vows of fidelity. A pledge of trust was made.

When Joseph was offered an illicit dalliance with another man's wife, his mind was fixed, not on fantasies of pleasures to come, but with the woman's husband, Potiphar, his employer. Joseph recited to Potiphar's wife (and perhaps to himself) the details of how kindly he had been treated. And so refusing to commit adultery was not just a cold moral decision, a choice between right or wrong, but an act of loyalty in the cherished relationship.

When temptation comes, heart and hormones battle to win the internal struggle we face. So when we are in that moment, perhaps we should remember to be not only obedient, but loyal as well, reminding ourselves that what we do has consequences and may cause great, lingering hurt to the people we love. Increasingly, vows are treated as disposable in our day. While there are many faithful and self-sacrificing public servants, some politicians take a solemn vow of office and then routinely lie and "spin the truth" (another phrase for "lie"). An oath is sworn in court, and then without hesitation the guilty party denies wrongdoing.

When tempted, let's not concentrate on the promise of pleasure to come, but remember the promises we have made in the past.

Pray: May love and faithfulness be mine when I am lured toward betraying You or others that I love. Amen.

Day 2. Potiphar's Wife: Sin against God

Read: Genesis 39:1–9; Psalm 51:1–19

Focus: "How then could I do such a wicked thing and sin against God?" (Gen. 39:9).

Sin is not a word found on many people's lips these days, especially among those who are not people of faith. We still recognize wrong, but tend to think about morality in terms of the results of certain actions; things are wrong because they damage the environment, wound others, or because the action causes us personal harm. But sin, which is obviously a concept found throughout the biblical narrative, goes beyond all these effects and points us to a God who is affected by our sin. Far from being stoic and unmoved, God's heart breaks over His world, and when we routinely persist in sinful behaviors, we hurt the God who loves us so. We see this "sinning against God" in the story of the decadent people of Sodom, as well as in David's treacherous behavior with Bathsheba and his plotting to have her husband killed (Ps. 51:4).

Not only does Joseph call Potiphar's wife out for her attempted seduction—it's not a little flirtation, some harmless fun, but rather great wickedness—but he refuses to sin, not only against her husband, but also against the Lord, who has been faithful to him.

It's been said that Christian obedience can be transactional—we woodenly obey because it's the right thing to do. But the Bible points us to *love for God* as the core motive for right living. We obey, not to be loved, but because we are loved, and we don't want to wound the One who loves us so. Anything less is just cold moralism. Today, we are loved. Let's not grieve the One who loves us.

Pray: Your care for me means that I can grieve You, Lord. Save me from that today. Amen.

Day 3. Potiphar's Wife: Potiphar–Negligent?

Read: Genesis 39:1–6; Ephesians 5:21–33

Focus: "So Potiphar left everything he had in Joseph's care; with Joseph in charge, he did not concern himself with anything except the food he ate" (Gen. 39:6).

It's easy to write off Potiphar's wife as a sex-crazed temptress who was just hungry for an afternoon of illicit pleasure—and who misused her powerful position by potentially exploiting one of her household staff. And perhaps it is as straightforward as that: sexual temptation carries very strong power.

But some commentators have noticed that Potiphar is described as someone who didn't bother about the details of his household, but was only concerned with what was on the menu. While this might just be a detail about how much he trusted Joseph, it's possible that the story is hinting that Potiphar was very concerned about his own needs, and especially the needs of his stomach, but failed to give attention to other areas. Perhaps Potiphar was also ignoring the needs of his wife, which gave her reason to look elsewhere. None of this justifies her actions, but it's just possible that they give us some insight as to why she acted as she did.

As with all relationships, marriage takes investment. Our relationships, be they with others in the local church, in our wider friendship circle, or in our family lives, all need to be maintained. Without the investment of time, attention, and some patience, relationships will erode.

Pray: Father, help me to never take those I love for granted. May I continue to give of myself, that love and friendship might truly last. Amen.

Day 4. Potiphar's Wife: Run for Your Life

Read: Genesis 39:1–12; 2 Timothy 2:22

Focus: "She caught him by his cloak and said, 'Come to bed with me!' But he left his cloak in her hand and ran out of the house" (Gen. 39:12).

Temptation comes to us all, and as we've seen, the lure of something that we know is wrong can be ongoing, nagging away at us, wearing us down. And there's an additional challenge: the temptation to flirt with temptation itself. We edge closer to what is a moral cliff edge, all the time telling ourselves that we can draw back and return to safety any time we want. But Joseph shows us that ultimately there's only one way to deal with temptation, and Potiphar's wife. His time for talking, refusing, professing loyalty, even affirming that he would not sin against God had come to an end. It was time to just run, to get out of the house, even if he left his cloak behind, which would be later used as evidence for false accusation.

I once knew a Christian leader who had a recurring problem with pornography, and so he refused to stay in a hotel room where there was a television that connected with online pornography—and sadly, most hotels offer horrible, so-called adult entertainment these days. Arriving at a hotel late one night, the maintenance department was closed for the day, and he was left in the room with a connected television. So he cut the cable, and then the next day, he went to the reception and paid for a replacement cable before checking out. Radical steps indeed, but he did what he felt he needed to do to ensure that he didn't plunge back into what had been an addiction for him. Is there a situation where we're lingering, rationalizing, discussing, but now it's time to simply … run?

Pray: Show me where I need to stop talking and start running, Lord. Amen.

Day 5. Potiphar's Wife: Shrugging Off Shame?

Read: Genesis 39:13–20; Galatians 5:14–15

Focus: "Then she told him this story: 'That Hebrew slave you brought us came to me to make sport of me. But as soon as I screamed for help, he left his cloak beside me and ran out of the house'" (Gen. 39:17–18).

Her behavior was shocking. Not only did she brazenly and recently pursue an adulterous relationship, but then, when refused, she accused Joseph. And her accusation was calculated, a carefully woven series of lies. She was the would-be seducer, but then suggested that Joseph had attempted rape. She screamed after Joseph ran, but when she told the story to her servants and then to her husband, she made out that it was her "scream for help" that caused him to run. And then the subtlety went even deeper, because in her report to her husband, she reminded him that Joseph was "that Hebrew slave you brought us … this is how your slave treated me." In other words, not only was this a false accusation, but Potiphar's wife managed to cast blame on everyone else—Joseph, and even her husband—in the way she told the story.

I've seen modern versions of this. People go looking to uncover the sins of others (and even sometimes falsely accuse them), and then later it's revealed that they themselves were guilty of that very sin.

Let's tell the truth—and when we get it wrong, own the blame.

Pray: Save me from being one who blames others for my own sins. And when I fail, help me to own my failure and receive Your grace. Amen.

Day 6. Potiphar's Wife: Joseph Shines Brightly

Read: Genesis 39:20–23; Philippians 2:12–18

Focus: "But while Joseph was there in the prison, the LORD was with him; he showed him kindness and granted him favor in the eyes of the prison warden" (Gen. 39:20–21).

Some people stand out because of their goodness. A few months ago, my church community were privileged to meet one of those quiet heroes, as we heard from Father Ubald, a Roman Catholic priest from Rwanda. Living through the horrors of the genocide, not only did he witness Christians killing Christians, but he lost forty-five thousand of his parishioners as well as eighty members of his own family, including his mother. But what a contrast the man is to the awful behavior he suffered. Meeting the killer of his mother in prison, he found out that the murderer's children were now orphans, because their mother had died. And so Father Ubald decided to adopt them both and pay for their education. The next year, one of them graduated as a doctor of medicine. What a glorious contrast to the darkness, to the venomous vengeance and violence that is genocide.

Before we leave this story of Potiphar's wife, we should remember that Joseph went to prison because of her false accusation. In a way, that's surprising, because usually the death penalty would have been exacted in the culture; perhaps it's an indication that Potiphar wasn't totally convinced by his wife's story. But once again Joseph was suffering terrible injustice, yet we hear no complaint from him, and again, we're told that God was with him in the midst of it all.

Following God is no guarantee that life will be easy. But today, albeit in smaller contexts, may we follow in the footsteps of the beautiful grace shown by Father Ubald, and the patient suffering of Joseph, and shine like stars in the darkness.

Pray: Fill me afresh with Your Holy Spirit today, that my life might shine for You, risen Jesus. Amen.

SAUL THE PERSECUTOR

The Call to Ongoing Change and Community

CONNECTING WITH ONE ANOTHER

If you had the opportunity to change one thing about you—physically, or in your temperament—what would it be?

KEY THOUGHT THIS SESSION

Sometimes we can be tempted to surrender to sameness; we believe that change is impossible for us. But as followers of Jesus, change is not just possible, but inevitable.

SCRIPTURE TO READ

Acts 26:1–23

Then Agrippa said to Paul, "You may speak in your defense."

So Paul, gesturing with his hand, started his defense: "I am fortunate, King Agrippa, that you are the one hearing my defense today against all these accusations made by the Jewish leaders, for I know you are an expert on all Jewish customs and controversies. Now please listen to me patiently!

"As the Jewish leaders are well aware, I was given a thorough Jewish training from my earliest childhood among my own people and in Jerusalem. If they would admit it, they know that I have been a member of the Pharisees, the strictest sect of our religion. Now I am on trial because of my hope in the fulfillment of God's promise made to our ancestors. In fact, that is why the twelve tribes of Israel zealously worship God night and day, and they share the same hope I have. Yet, Your Majesty, they accuse me for having this hope! Why does it seem incredible to any of you that God can raise the dead?

"I used to believe that I ought to do everything I could to oppose the very name of Jesus the Nazarene. Indeed, I did just that in Jerusalem. Authorized by the leading priests, I caused many believers there to be sent to prison. And I cast my vote against them when they were condemned to death. Many times I had them punished in the synagogues to get them to curse Jesus. I was so violently opposed to them that I even chased them down in foreign cities.

"One day I was on such a mission to Damascus, armed with the authority and commission of the leading priests. About noon, Your Majesty, as I was on the road, a light from heaven brighter than the sun shone down on me and my companions. We all fell down, and I heard a voice saying to me in Aramaic, 'Saul, Saul, why are you persecuting me? It is useless for you to fight against my will.'

"'Who are you, lord?' I asked.

"And the Lord replied, 'I am Jesus, the one you are persecuting. Now get to your feet! For I have appeared to you to appoint you as my servant and witness. Tell people that you have seen me, and tell them what I will show you in the future. And I will rescue you from both your own people and the Gentiles. Yes, I am sending you to the Gentiles to open their eyes, so they may turn from darkness to light and from the power of Satan to God. Then they will receive forgiveness for their sins and be given a place among God's people, who are set apart by faith in me.'

"And so, King Agrippa, I obeyed that vision from heaven. I preached first to those in Damascus,

then in Jerusalem and throughout all Judea, and
also to the Gentiles, that all must repent of their sins
and turn to God—and prove they have changed by
the good things they do. Some Jews arrested me
in the Temple for preaching this, and they tried to
kill me. But God has protected me right up to this
present time so I can testify to everyone, from the
least to the greatest. I teach nothing except what
the prophets and Moses said would happen—
that the Messiah would suffer and be the first to
rise from the dead, and in this way announce God's
light to Jews and Gentiles alike." (NLT)

Acts 22:6–10

About noon as I came near Damascus, suddenly a
bright light from heaven flashed around me. I fell
to the ground and heard a voice say to me, "Saul!
Saul! Why do you persecute me?"

"Who are you, Lord?" I asked.

"I am Jesus of Nazareth, whom you are persecuting," he replied. My companions saw the light,
but they did not understand the voice of him who
was speaking to me.

"What shall I do, Lord?" I asked.

"Get up," the Lord said, "and go into
Damascus. There you will be told all that you have
been assigned to do."

James 4:13–17

> Now listen, you who say, "Today or tomorrow
> we will go to this or that city, spend a year there,
> carry on business and make money." Why, you do
> not even know what will happen tomorrow. What
> is your life? You are a mist that appears for a little
> while and then vanishes. Instead, you ought to say,
> "If it is the Lord's will, we will live and do this or
> that." As it is, you boast in your arrogant schemes.
> All such boasting is evil. If anyone, then, knows the
> good they ought to do and doesn't do it, it is sin
> for them.

FOR YOUR CONSIDERATION

As far as the believers in the early church were concerned, there was
one man who was perhaps the least likely to convert to Christ—and
his name was Saul. We look back and see that Saul became the great
apostle Paul, planting churches and giving us a third of the New
Testament. But those early believers saw him as the passionate, evil
enemy of the faith, a catalyst for the persecution that caused the
Jerusalem Christians to scatter, losing their homes, businesses, and
in some cases, their lives. Change for him seemed unlikely, impossible even, but it happened. Saul's story gives us hope when we are
tempted to give up on people who are making a mess of their lives, or
are just resistant to the gospel: God can meet with them. And there's
hope for us as well, because if Saul can change, then so can we.

But for the Christian, change is not just about resolution and determination—gritting our teeth and doing our best. We *do* need to make good choices, but we are not alone in the pursuit of change. Christianity is not just about embracing a "holy" code, but allowing the power of a holy God to fill us each day. Change is not just revising our outward behavior, but heart change that comes when we navigate life with the Lord.

Paul experienced that, and wrote about it:

> Dear friends, you always followed my instructions when I was with you. And now that I am away, it is even more important. Work hard to show the results of your salvation, obeying God with deep reverence and fear. For God is working in you, giving you the desire and the power to do what pleases him. (Phil. 2:12–13 NLT)

In these few sentences, Paul shows that we are called to be partners with God in the process of change—we work, and He works in us. But just how does He do that work?

First of all, the Holy Spirit is the One who convicts us. There are promptings that come, not just because we have been raised with a moral code, or because of conscience, but because God is nudging us (and using that code and conscience) to show us the error of our ways. Through this, He lovingly brings us to repentance, grace, and healthy living. Saul experienced that. And that work had been going on in Saul's heart before he ever set out on his trip to Damascus. When Jesus said to Saul, "It is useless for you to fight against my will," many translations, including the New International Version, say, "It is hard for you to kick against the goads" (Acts 26:14).

Goads were used to control oxen, to break them in. So what was the goad in Saul's experience? Perhaps it was the fact that Saul would have heard of Jesus' work and miracles. He had seen the resilience of the Christians who were willing to face prison and even death rather than renounce their Lord. He had seen the light on Stephen's face as he died an agonizing death, and heard Stephen's prayer that his executioners might be forgiven. And Saul had heard Stephen's dying outburst that he could see Jesus. All that, coupled with a conscience that surely pricked him too, and we see that Jesus was relentlessly pursuing Saul.

Sometimes we kick against the goads when we willfully pursue a pathway that we know is contrary to the will of God. Conscience pains us. While we know that the conscience is fallible—some people have a hypersensitive attitude that makes them feel bad even when they have done nothing wrong—let's be sensitive to those twinges and never kick against those goads. As Jesus said to Saul, it's hard work to do so.

In surrendering to the convicting work of God, Saul then made himself available to Jesus and His purposes, in asking two questions of Jesus: Who are You, and what should I do?

Life brings lots of questions. What should I do for a career? Where should I live? If I'm to marry, then whom? Which church community should I be a part of?

The conversion of Saul brings us back to the two *most important* questions of life. In the various tellings of his turnaround moment, we see that the first question he asked was of Jesus: Who are You? If

Jesus truly is the Son of God, the One crucified for us, the victor over the grave, then life is radically different. Being a Christian in response to that question is not some vague, wooly thing, a dab of faith to get us through the tough times. Jesus is Lord, and as we understand that, we turn our lives over fully to His kingdom purposes. And that leads us to the second question Saul asked: What should I do?

Now that we know who Jesus is, our lives are not our own. And having turned over the reins of our lives to Him, we don't want to take them back. James warns against gradually developing an independent attitude where our plans are our own, made without consultation or submission to God. Who He is leads us to ask what we should do in response to Him being Lord and King. Perhaps the second question is one that some of us used to ask but haven't lately: What should I do for and with You, Lord? As we do that, and genuinely wait before Him, determined to do His will, we find purpose and peace.

Author Brennan Manning wrote:

> Today I double up with laughter whenever I realize that I have started "managing" my own life once more—something we all do with astounding regularity. The illusion of control is truly pathetic, but it is also hilarious. Deciding what I most need out of life, carefully calculating my next move, and generally allowing my autonomous self to run amuck inflates my sense of self-importance and reduces the God of my incredible journey to the role of spectator on the sidelines. It is only the wisdom and perspective gleaned from an hour of silent prayer

each morning that prevents me from running for
CEO of the universe. As Henri Nouwen once
remarked, "One of the most arduous spiritual tasks
is that of giving up control and allowing the Spirit
of God to lead our lives."[1]

Saul also experienced the power of change as he gave himself to
Christian community, the church. This wasn't easy for him. When he
first tried to align himself with the believers in Jerusalem, they were
terrified of him, thinking that he might be a spy—the persecutor
up to his old, terrible tricks. It was only when Barnabas intervened
that Saul was finally welcomed. But it was in the company of those
believers that Saul discovered his apostolic calling and destiny.

When he came to Jerusalem, he tried to join the
disciples, but they were all afraid of him, not believing that he really was a disciple. But Barnabas took
him and brought him to the apostles. He told them
how Saul on his journey had seen the Lord and that
the Lord had spoken to him, and how in Damascus
he had preached fearlessly in the name of Jesus. So
Saul stayed with them and moved about freely in
Jerusalem, speaking boldly in the name of the Lord.
(Acts 9:26–28)

Some Christians treat church as an optional extra, even boasting
that "the mountains are my church." Or church becomes like an
extension of a house rather than a foundation for it.

Author Michael Griffiths wrote:

> Pick up a hymn book … note how very many "I" and "my" hymns there are, and how relatively few "we" and "our" hymns there are, which are really suitable for congregational singing. Most of our hymns would be more suitable as solos! It is as if most Christians expect to fly solo to heaven with only just a little bit of formation flying from time to time.[2]

But solo Christianity is not what we're called to. We grow, we learn, we change, and we discover purpose together.

If you are using the DVD, watch session 4.

STUDY AND DISCUSSION

1. Imagine if you had been there when Saul tried to meet with the Jerusalem believers. Would you have been nervous and reluctant, or open to welcome him?

2. What are some of the more significant changes that have taken place in your life as a follower of Jesus?

3. "Having turned over the reins of our lives to Him, we don't want to take them back." How might we "take our lives back"? How can we prevent that from happening?

GOING DEEPER

"Most people do not really want freedom, because freedom involves responsibility, and most people are frightened by responsibility."[3] Discuss this thought.

Or:

"And then the day came when the risk to remain tight, in a bud, became more painful than the risk it took to blossom."[4] What risks have you taken to "blossom"? Why is "remaining tight in a bud" sometimes very risky?

THIS SESSION'S CHALLENGE

Pray this prayer each morning: "Lord, what would You like me to do?"

DAILY BIBLE NOTES: SAUL
Day 1. Saul the Persecutor

Read: Galatians 1:11–24; Romans 1:16–17

Focus: "For you have heard of my previous way of life in Judaism, how intensely I persecuted the church of God and tried to destroy it" (Gal. 1:13).

It's a question that we all ask at times, especially when we're frustrated with ourselves or get stuck in negative patterns of behavior.

After a while, we wonder: Can we really change, or are we sentenced to sameness?

The Christian answer to that question is that genuine change is a reality through Christ. And the uncomfortable reality that so many Christians seem to get stuck in—changing initially and then settling down—doesn't change this truth: walk with Jesus and change will happen.

The story of one of the archvillains of the New Testament, Saul, shows us the true power of transformation that the good news of Jesus brings. The mention of the name Saul would have provoked fear in those early Christians trying to be faithful to Christ in Jerusalem. As we'll unpack in these daily Bible notes, he oversaw a terrible campaign against those beleaguered believers. Nobody could have ever imagined the utter revolution that would come into his life, as the persecutor became the apostle. But it happened. A third of the New Testament would flow from his pen. Churches were planted. Nations shaken. But it wasn't just that Saul's behavior changed: he became a new man, with a new heart and a reason for living—and dying. Paul changed. And so can we, God helping us.

Pray: You are the God of miracles and transformation. Work Your wonders in and through me, even today. Amen.

Day 2. Dealing with Our Greatest Regrets

Read: Acts 7:54–8:1; 22:20

Focus: "And Saul approved of their killing him" (Acts 8:1).

Here's a question that might provoke some soul searching: What's the worst thing that you've ever done? We are all deeply flawed, and most of us have episodes along the way that we regret. We wish we could turn back the clock and undo the hurt that our actions have caused others, and ourselves.

Luke wrote about Stephen's death and Saul's participation in the awful execution, and there's no attempt to gloss over the horror of it all. Apparently stoning a healthy person to death takes a lot of protracted effort and energy—it's hot and physically exerting work, hence those who took part removed their coats. As guardian of the coats, it's possible that Saul also acted as a herald, summoning others to join in or watch the bloody spectacle. And lest we be in any doubt, Luke revealed Saul's thinking as well as his actions: he thoroughly approved of the stoning.

So why such gross detail? Perhaps Luke crafted his description this way to show us just how horrendous Saul's sin was. And Saul/Paul would later describe himself as a "chief of sinners," in no doubt about his crime, and perhaps tormented by the memory of it.

Let's go back to that question about the worst sin you've ever committed. However bad it was, God's forgiveness is freely available. Saul probably struggled to forgive himself for his role in Stephen's death. Even grace could not undo the damage and reverse the loss. But he refused to be paralyzed by his past: the man who received grace preached grace.

Pray: I bring my deepest regrets, my greatest shame to You, forgiving Father. Help me to not just believe in Your grace, but also to live in it. Amen.

Day 3. A Ferocious Attack

Read: Acts 8:1–3; Galatians 1:11–14

Focus: "But Saul began to destroy the church. Going from house to house, he dragged off both men and women and put them in prison" (Acts 8:3).

I've mentioned often that some Christian television is bad for my blood pressure, especially when a smiling huckster promises health, wealth, and an easy life. No such promises are made in the Gospels, and the terrible hardships that the early church suffered make it clear: following Jesus is not a ticket to a stress-free life. In writing about the terrible persecution that was launched by the martyrdom of Stephen, Luke used words that clearly capture a sense of their pain. Describing the ferocity of Saul's attack on the church, Luke chose a word that is often used to describe an attack of a wild beast, tearing its prey limb from limb. And then Luke wanted us to know that women as well as men were victims in the horrors, a fact that is alluded to twice more in the book of Acts (9:2; 22:4).

While there are many around the world who suffer terribly for their faith in Christ, we know very little about that here in the West. But it is true that Christians seem to be fair game for acerbic humor. Recently the renowned British evangelist J. John wrote an open letter to the BBC, gently pointing out a very clear bias that there seems to be against Christians. It's hardly persecution, but we should know that the decision to follow Jesus is increasingly likely to create a negative reaction, especially if we make ethical choices that are not pleasing to the mainstream consensus. Following Christ can be tough, but let's remember that it was that way at the beginning too.

Pray: Strengthen all Your people, and strengthen me, Lord, when following You is costly. Amen.

Day 4. Obsession and Shame

Read: Acts 26:1–11; 1 Timothy 1:15–16

Focus: "Here is a trustworthy saying that deserves full acceptance: Christ Jesus came into the world to save sinners—of whom I am the worst" (1 Tim. 1:15).

So now we have a composite picture of the man that was Saul the persecutor before he became Paul the apostle—who targeted women as well as men in his rampage against the church. But the picture is not complete, because now Paul himself tells us that he was "obsessed" with attacking Christians; this is the warped zeal of a white-hot fanatic. Perhaps this is another reason why Paul describes himself as "the worst of sinners." Elsewhere he calls himself "the least of the apostles" (1 Cor. 15:9) and "less than the least of all the Lord's people" (Eph. 3:8). He repeatedly makes reference to his sins.

I mentioned earlier that Paul might have struggled to fully accept forgiveness for the terrible things that he'd done, even though he did them in ignorance, believing that he was serving God zealously. But then maybe Paul knew that it was important for him to never forget where he came from and what he was before he met Christ. He would become a revered leader in the early church, and as we've seen, the author of a third of the New Testament. Remembering his own horrible history surely helped him maintain genuine humility, as he recognized that anything he achieved was through God's grace. He called the feuding Corinthians to remember what they were before Jesus saved them, insisting that "God chose the foolish things of the world to shame the wise; God chose the weak things of the world to shame the strong" (1 Cor. 1:27). When we're tempted to be proud, we should look back with gratitude and humility.

Pray: When blessing and success come, help me to remember that You alone are my Savior and Source, Lord Jesus. Amen.

Day 5. Redeemer

Read: Acts 8:1–4; 11:19–24

Focus: "Those who had been scattered preached the word wherever they went" (Acts 8:4).

It's a truth that I often celebrate and thank God for—His beautiful ability to redeem, to take circumstances that He did not will or design, episodes of evil, but then turn them around for good. We see this pattern repeatedly through biblical history. It's hard to comprehend how something good could come out of the terrible atrocities committed by Paul when he was Saul—but then with God, all things are possible. The persecution scattered the believers far and wide, displacing them from homes, families, and businesses, with shattering social and economic consequences. Caught up in such chaos, it would have been impossible to see anything very positive about it. But as we pan the camera of history back, we see that Saul's plan to destroy the church backfired because of redemption: the displaced believers talked about Jesus as they traveled, spreading the good news far and wide and leading to revival in Samaria and the birthing of the mainly gentile church in Antioch. Yet again, God turned for good that which was intended for evil. Can you think of a situation where God turned something bad around for good in your life?

Pray: I praise You, Lord, because not only do You forgive sin, but You sometimes bring good even out of my foolishness. This does not nudge me to more sin, but rather to deep gratitude. Amen.

Day 6. He Identifies with Us

Read: Acts 9:1–9; Jeremiah 32:37–41

It's happened more than a few times. I've unexpectedly found myself in a situation where it is embarrassing to be identified as a Christian. The conversation is sophisticated around the dinner table, and unaware that I'm a believer and the nature of what I do, faith is mocked as a crutch for the weak. And then comes the question: "What do you think, Jeff?" Or yet another major scandal rocks the worldwide church, and scorn is poured on the many because of the base behavior of the few. Suddenly I don't want to line up with the Christians. But Saul's stunning conversion shows us this wonderful, challenging truth: Jesus is not ashamed of us. On the contrary …

The account of the conversion is incredible. The archenemy of the church, Saul, was brought to his knees as he encountered the awesome power of the risen Jesus. Revolution on the Damascus Road. But as Jesus spoke to Saul—surely a terrifying experience, considering the damage Saul had done to His church—Jesus totally identifies Himself with His people. Persecuting them was tantamount to persecuting *Him*.

And for all the terrible failures and foibles of the church throughout history, where God has both been glorified and smeared because of the actions of His people, Jesus still aligns Himself with us. We are His. Seeing as He is not ashamed of us with all our flaws, surely we should not be ashamed of Him in His perfection. Today, with kindness and grace, line up with Jesus and His people.

Pray: When opportunity comes, help me to stand as one unashamed of You, Lord Jesus. Thank You for Your faithfulness to me. Amen.

MICHAL, DAUGHTER OF KING SAUL

The Call to Kindness

CONNECTING WITH ONE ANOTHER

Describe your closest, longest friendship. What has helped sustain it through the years?

KEY THOUGHT THIS SESSION

All relationships need investment and, at times, repair. When we live in a place of constant, critical fruitlessness—and bitterness leads to barrenness—we're called to live kind, gracious lives.

SCRIPTURE TO READ

1 Samuel 18:20–21

Now Saul's daughter Michal was in love with David, and when they told Saul about it, he was pleased. "I will give her to him," he thought, "so that she may be a snare to him and so that the hand of the Philistines may be against him." So Saul said to David, "Now you have a second opportunity to become my son-in-law."

2 Samuel 6:12–23

Now King David was told, "The LORD has blessed the household of Obed-Edom and everything he has, because of the ark of God." So David went to bring up the ark of God from the house of Obed-Edom to the City of David with rejoicing. When those who were carrying the ark of the LORD had taken six steps, he sacrificed a bull and a fattened calf. Wearing a linen ephod, David was dancing before the LORD with all his might, while he and all Israel were bringing up the ark of the LORD with shouts and the sound of trumpets.

As the ark of the LORD was entering the City of David, Michal daughter of Saul watched from a window. And when she saw King David leaping and dancing before the LORD, she despised him in her heart.

They brought the ark of the LORD and set it in its place inside the tent that David had pitched for it, and David sacrificed burnt offerings and fellowship offerings before the LORD. After he had finished sacrificing the burnt offerings and fellowship offerings, he blessed the people in the name of the LORD Almighty. Then he gave a loaf of bread, a cake of dates and a cake of raisins to each person in the whole crowd of Israelites, both men and women. And all the people went to their homes.

When David returned home to bless his household, Michal daughter of Saul came out to meet him and said, "How the king of Israel has distinguished himself today, going around half-naked in full view of the slave girls of his servants as any vulgar fellow would!"

David said to Michal, "It was before the LORD, who chose me rather than your father or anyone from his house when he appointed me ruler over the LORD's people Israel—I will celebrate before the LORD. I will become even more undignified than this, and I will be humiliated in my own eyes. But by these slave girls you spoke of, I will be held in honor."

And Michal daughter of Saul had no children to the day of her death.

Galatians 5:22–23

But the fruit of the Spirit is love, joy, peace, forbearance, kindness, goodness, faithfulness, gentleness and self-control.

FOR YOUR CONSIDERATION

Earlier in our journey together we gave some consideration to worship, as we reflected on the story of Cain and Abel. This session we look at what should have been a time of united national celebration, as after some disastrous previous attempt, the Ark of the Covenant was finally brought home at the order of King David.

Anything can be criticized, no matter how good it is. King David's act of worship was very extravagant and deliberate—every six steps the procession into the city stopped and fresh offerings were made. And it was a joyful, even boisterous celebration; when we read that David "danced before the Lord," the Hebrew means "to separate the limbs." Volume was high too. Most of all, it was accepted by God—again, as we've seen before, worship is not about style or preference.

But one member of the royal family was not amused. We're told that David's wife, Michal, "despised" David.

While nation and king celebrated the joyous occasion, Michal sulked as though former king Saul would have done better. But she had forgotten that Saul had neglected the ark (and God!) and refused to heed the warnings of the prophet Samuel.[1]

The picture that we have of Michal is one of angst and bitterness, but it had not always been that way. Twice in 1 Samuel 18 we hear of her love for David. But whatever the cause of her bitter and critical attitudes, things had changed, and the exchange between husband and wife showed that all was not well in their relationship. Both Michal and David were somewhat acerbic and sarcastic in their comments back and forth.

Relational harmony doesn't just happen. Friendship calls for investment. Marriage takes time and sacrifice. And unity in the local church needs to be maintained, lest harmony and togetherness are eroded.

Perhaps some of us are on "cruise control" in a relationship, assuming that all will be well because all has been well in the past. Let's not assume too much, and let's move quickly to mend breaches in our relationships, lest we find them deteriorating beyond possible repair in days to come. Better to invest today than attempt to repair tomorrow.

And sometimes we can be wrong—when we're partly right. One commentator noted that David might have been somewhat immodest as he got carried away with enthusiasm:

> Perhaps during his frenzied movements in the dance the linen ephod which he was wearing slipped from his body so that his nakedness could be seen. In a state of ecstasy such happenings were not uncommon (cf. 1 Sam. 19:24). Israelite law forbids priests to expose their nakedness in holy places (Exod. 20:26). Exposing one's nakedness openly was taboo in Israel (cf. Gen. 9:22ff.; Lev. 18:6ff.). David's ecstatic behavior was typical of Canaanite practice, and that could have been one reason why Michal could not appreciate it. David justified his behavior as self-abasement before the LORD, as an expression of his gratitude to God for all that God had done for him (2 Sam. 6:21–22).[2]

We can be right about an issue, but wrong in the way we communicate our concern about that issue. And some people make a continual habit of being critical:

> These people are grumblers and faultfinders; they follow their own evil desires; they boast about themselves and flatter others for their own advantage. (Jude v. 16)

The original word for "grumblers" here is associated with the cooing of doves; like birds that never stop repeating the same noise, people who find fault always seem to follow the same script!

It's also possible that Michal was angry because she had been treated as a commodity, even by David:

> "But I demand one thing of you: Do not come into my presence unless you bring Michal daughter of Saul when you come to see me." Then David sent messengers to Ish-Bosheth son of Saul, demanding, "Give me my wife Michal, whom I betrothed to myself for the price of a hundred Philistine foreskins."
>
> So Ish-Bosheth gave orders and had her taken away from her husband Paltiel son of Laish. Her husband, however, went with her, weeping behind her all the way to Bahurim. Then Abner said to him, "Go back home!" So he went back. (2 Sam. 3:13–16)

But while we cannot choose the circumstances of life, we can choose how we will respond to them.

With her critical attitude, Michal was childless for the rest of her life. Here we need to tread very carefully, because mishandling this episode could hurt those who battle childlessness. There is absolutely no suggestion that an inability to have children is the result of judgment upon some sin. But in Michal's specific case, it appears that might have been an act of judgment, although we can't be sure. It might just be that a son of Michal's would have been a grandson of Saul's, which could have led to a clash of dynasties. It might also be that David withdrew from an ongoing sexual relationship with her from this time on. What we do know is that living a cynical, complaining life bears no good fruit, and to continue the metaphor, a root of bitterness can defile others (Heb. 12:15).

In *Shoah*, Claude Lanzmann's documentary on the Holocaust, a leader of a Warsaw ghetto uprising speaks of the bitterness that remains in his soul over how he and his people were treated by the Nazis. "If you could lick my heart, it would poison you."

By contrast, in her care for fellow Holocaust survivors, Corrie ten Boom saw the power of ongoing bitterness tragically demonstrated. She learned that forgiveness was a daily act and that those who had found grace to forgive their former enemies were able to return to a sense of normality again and rebuild their lives, even when their physical scars were extreme. But those who, to use her phrase, "nursed their bitterness" remained dysfunctional. Corrie affirmed, "It was as simple and as horrible as that."

Philip Yancey's description of the books of two Nobel Prize–winning writers illustrates the power of "ungrace" and bitterness.[3] *Love in the Time of Cholera*, by Gabriel García Márquez, chronicles a marriage that disintegrates over the failure of the wife to put a bar of soap out for her husband! "Even when they were old ... they were careful about bringing it up, for the barely healed wounds could begin to bleed again as if they had been only inflicted yesterday."[4] *The Knot of Vipers* by François Mauriac tells of another marriage breakdown, perpetuated by a husband and wife who both wait for the other to initiate grace and forgiveness—in vain.[5] Neither one ever breaks the cycle of gracelessness and forgives. The decision to forgive others who have hurt us is not just for their benefit: there is a sense of self-preservation about forgiveness, as failure to forgive will produce toxic effects in our own lives, including an inability really to accept God's grace for our failings.

Let's live kind, gracious, generous lives.

If you are using the DVD, watch session 5.

STUDY AND DISCUSSION

1. What kind of investment do we need to make into our relationships?
2. What advice would you give to a person who struggles to forgive?
3. Why is bitterness so destructive?

GOING DEEPER

Writer Emmet Fox said, "Criticism is an indirect form of self-boasting." What does this mean? Do you agree?

Or:

Minister Charles Finney once said, "A censorious spirit is conclusive evidence of a backslidden heart … it is a state of mind that reveals itself in harsh judgments, harsh sayings, and the manifestation of uncomfortable feelings towards individuals. This state of mind is entirely incompatible with a loving heart."[6] Discuss this perspective.

THIS SESSION'S CHALLENGE

Ask the Holy Spirit to show you any situations in your life where kindness has become a casualty. Then intentionally invest in one or two friendships—you can give your time, a word of encouragement, or an unexpected gift, for examples.

DAILY BIBLE NOTES: MICHAL
Day 1. Michal, Daughter of Saul

Read: 2 Samuel 6:1–16; Proverbs 16:18

Focus: "As the ark of the LORD was entering the City of David, Michal daughter of Saul watched from a window. And when she saw King David leaping and dancing before the LORD, she despised him in her heart" (2 Sam. 6:16).

It happens when we Christians find ourselves in an unfamiliar church context. People are worshipping the Lord in a way that is unfamiliar to us—their style is not our style. I'm grateful for my Pentecostal heritage, but I was rather convinced that our exuberant style, with occasional hands raised, hand clapping, and "Amen" and "Praise the Lord" peppering the sermon, was the only way to worship. Getting involved in wider cross-denominational ministry showed me how arrogant I'd become. I thought I was holy, but I was haughty. And since then, I have had the privilege of ministering in so many different expressions of the Christian family: tuba-playing salvationists, Mennonites singing five-part harmonies unaccompanied, and Anglo-Catholics wafting incense and sprinkling holy water around.

Michal might not exactly be a villain, but I include her in this group because she did stand squarely against David in a strategic episode of worship, and apparently was judged heavily for doing so. As we'll see over the next few days, she sinned by assuming the posture of a critical spectator of worship rather than a willing participator. There are complex reasons for her stance, but for now, let's realize that there are others in the Christian family who express their faith in vastly different ways from our own styles, but who love Jesus no less than we do—and probably, in some cases, more than we do.

Pray: Lord, grant me humility when others approach worship and Christian faith with styles and thinking unfamiliar to me. Amen.

Day 2. Spectators in Church

Read: 2 Samuel 6:16; Ephesians 4:1–13

Focus: "As the ark of the LORD was entering the City of David, Michal daughter of Saul watched from a window" (2 Sam. 6:16a).

It's a problem that is frequently referred to in internet articles. People are not joining in with the singing in worship like they used to. I love high-energy worship, with a great band playing. I've no objection to the big screens, the lights, the smoke. But the atmosphere can change from a worship experience where everyone is involved to a concert where we just stand and watch others perform. It's not that we don't enjoy the event, but our part in it has changed. And often, we're not even aware that the shift has taken place.

I've already mentioned that Michal acted like a spectator, and in tomorrow's Bible notes, we'll consider some possible reasons for that. Instead of getting involved in this celebration of thanksgiving to God, she watched from a window. And very quickly the spectator became a harsh critic. Something similar can happen to us; we can become worship spectators, always evaluating, critiquing, but not actually fully joining in.

Our personality types may well affect the way we express ourselves. But let's ensure that we participate fully as we engage in worship, be it in song, in financial giving, or whatever. The heart of worship is sacrifice, and the call to worship has always been to the community of God, not just the people who stand on the stage.

When you attend worship services and events, what's your stance? Paul's directive to the Ephesians to all serve as members of the body of Christ made it clear: we're called to be servants, not spectators.

Pray: Help me to fully engage as a member of Your body, Lord: in worship, in service, in giving. Amen.

Day 3. Judging Motives

Read: 2 Samuel 6:16; Jude verse 16

I've done it myself. During a worship gathering, I suddenly notice somebody who is being very expressive in their praise. Perhaps they're dancing wildly at the front, or shouting a little too loudly. Or it might be the other extreme that catches my attention—while everyone else is standing, they are sitting, refusing to sing, their faces wooden and sullen. I assume that the loud person is an attention seeker, and that the quiet soul is angry and even bitter. And I may be completely wrong in my assumptions.

Michal criticized David for what she viewed as unseemly behavior, especially for a king. Contrary to what some preachers say, David did not dance naked, but with a simple linen garment. Perhaps it slipped, and there was an immodest moment. That would not be good, especially as the law clearly forbade the exposure of nakedness in holy places (Ex. 20:26). And David's ecstatic worship was rather similar to the occult practices of the Canaanites. But his motives were right. Let's be slow to make judgments about others when they worship in ways that are not our own.

Speaker Zig Ziglar famously observed that some people find fault like there is a reward for it. Is there a style of worship that especially grates on you, and you quickly become irritated when you see it?

Pray: When finding fault seems like finding something valuable, guard my heart and my lips, Lord. Amen.

Day 4. Stuck in the Past

Read: 2 Samuel 6:16–20; 1 Samuel 18:1–21

Focus: "When David returned home to bless his household, Michal daughter of Saul came out to meet him" (2 Sam. 6:20).

It was a blast from the past, watching Michael J. Fox in *Back to the Future* recently. Fox plays a character who is transported back to the 1950s (from what now seems like the thoroughly out-of-date 1980s!) and is desperate to return to his own time. Assisted by a mad-professor character, he longs to get his life back.

While some of us hanker for the future, some of us live stranded in the past, weighed down by what was, by what we did, by decisions we made that can't be undone. There's evidence to suggest that Michal's angry and critical attitude was caused by her history. She was always known as "Michal, daughter of Saul" rather than "Michal, wife of David." Seemingly she was trapped in that identity. Some commentators have even suggested that this was a hint that she was acting as David's enemy rather than his wife.

Men, including her father, had not treated Michal well. When Saul found out that his daughter was in love with David, he was delighted and felt that she would be a snare to him—hardly warm approval. And her father was a violent, unpredictable man, given to sudden outbreaks of rage and throwing javelins around when the mood struck him.

We are all products of the past, and I would not want to minimize the very real damaging effects that our histories can have on us. But in

Christ, as we journey with Him, and perhaps seek counsel and professional help if needed, we are not stranded helplessly in the past.

Pray: Father, You know my journey. Where I need to take an ongoing journey of recovery from any aspects of my history, lead me forward with Your healing hand. Amen.

Day 5. Other People's Opinions

Read: 2 Samuel 6:21; 1 Corinthians 3:18–23

Focus: "David said to Michal, 'It was before the LORD, who chose me rather than your father or anyone from his house when he appointed me ruler over the LORD's people Israel—I will celebrate before the LORD'" (2 Sam. 6:21).

It's something that most of us struggle with at times: we worry about what people think of us. Concern about how I am perceived has led me to make some risky choices over the years. I once scuba dived in shark-infested waters where box jellyfish were a real danger. Thinking that I really didn't want to go through with the dive, I went ahead simply because I didn't want the others in the dive group (complete strangers whom I would never meet again) to think that I was being cowardly. I risked my life rather than risked looking silly in their eyes, even though I would never know their thoughts anyway. Over the years, standing on public platforms has brought its challenges. I like people to be happy with me. Like most, I like to be liked, but sometimes, the messenger has to bring unwelcome words, and risk criticism as a result. And all people of faith risk being written off as "fools" because they believe.

David refused to be shackled to Michal's opinion of his worship style. As we'll see in tomorrow's Bible notes, it's possible that he didn't respond perfectly to her sniping, but he determined that he would do what was honorable before God, even if it meant that only pious slaves would approve. What mattered was that he did the right thing, even if it meant that he was judged as being undignified.

Someone once said that we would worry less about what people think of us if we only knew how little time people spend thinking of us. That's not bad advice.

Pray: When I am excessively anxious about how others view me, help me to be confident, especially when I know I am being obedient to You. Amen.

Day 6. When You're Criticized

Read: 2 Samuel 6:22; Proverbs 27:6

Focus: "I will become even more undignified than this, and I will be humiliated in my own eyes. But by these slave girls you spoke of, I will be held in honor" (2 Sam. 6:22).

Talent judge Simon Cowell has built a huge entertainment business because of his critical gift. When he launched the first series of what are effectively glitzy talent shows, he stunned his audiences with his forthright, often cutting critiques of would-be "stars." We cringe at his bluntness; it seems cruel to tell people that they have no talent and trash their hopes and dreams. But while I'm not suggesting that we emulate his delivery style, we should know that criticism can be helpful, if we give it—and receive it—with kindness.

Michal's criticism of her husband was largely unjustified. She was questioning his motives as well as his style, suggesting that he was playing to the audience of slave girls rather than honoring the Lord. David did well in refusing to back off, and insisting that if worship meant humiliation, then he would worship anyway. But perhaps he went too far as he reminded Michal that God had blessed him and rejected her father, Saul. While I might be reading a little too much into his words, it seems that David might have responded to spite with spite, which is unhelpful. We don't have to bow to every harsh word spoken about us. Living means that criticism will be a reality for all of us. But we don't have to react either. When criticized, stay cool. There might be helpful truth in the criticism, even if the tone of the critic is hurtful. And if we're stung, let's be careful to not sting back. It's not easy, but it might prevent greater conflict.

Ponder: Is there a situation where you're being criticized helpfully but you're rejecting it because it stings?

JEZEBEL
The Call to Use Power and Influence Well

CONNECTING WITH ONE ANOTHER

Share briefly about one person who has had a significant impact and influence in your life—for good or bad (if it's bad, don't name the person!).

KEY THOUGHT THIS SESSION

We all have influence. How do we use it—to serve others, or to manipulate and control them? Manipulation is a subtle art. And who is influencing us now?

SCRIPTURE TO READ

1 Kings 16:29–33

In the thirty-eighth year of Asa king of Judah, Ahab
son of Omri became king of Israel, and he reigned
in Samaria over Israel twenty-two years. Ahab son
of Omri did more evil in the eyes of the LORD than
any of those before him. He not only considered
it trivial to commit the sins of Jeroboam son of
Nebat, but he also married Jezebel daughter of
Ethbaal king of the Sidonians, and began to serve
Baal and worship him. He set up an altar for Baal
in the temple of Baal that he built in Samaria. Ahab
also made an Asherah pole and did more to arouse
the anger of the LORD, the God of Israel, than did
all the kings of Israel before him.

1 Kings 19:1–3

Now Ahab told Jezebel everything Elijah had done
and how he had killed all the prophets with the
sword. So Jezebel sent a messenger to Elijah to say,
"May the gods deal with me, be it ever so severely, if
by this time tomorrow I do not make your life like
that of one of them."

Elijah was afraid and ran for his life.

1 Kings 21:1–19

Some time later there was an incident involving a
vineyard belonging to Naboth the Jezreelite. The

vineyard was in Jezreel, close to the palace of Ahab king of Samaria. Ahab said to Naboth, "Let me have your vineyard to use for a vegetable garden, since it is close to my palace. In exchange I will give you a better vineyard or, if you prefer, I will pay you whatever it is worth."

But Naboth replied, "The LORD forbid that I should give you the inheritance of my ancestors."

So Ahab went home, sullen and angry because Naboth the Jezreelite had said, "I will not give you the inheritance of my ancestors." He lay on his bed sulking and refused to eat.

His wife Jezebel came in and asked him, "Why are you so sullen? Why won't you eat?"

He answered her, "Because I said to Naboth the Jezreelite, 'Sell me your vineyard; or if you prefer, I will give you another vineyard in its place.' But he said, 'I will not give you my vineyard.'"

Jezebel his wife said, "Is this how you act as king over Israel? Get up and eat! Cheer up. I'll get you the vineyard of Naboth the Jezreelite."

So she wrote letters in Ahab's name, placed his seal on them, and sent them to the elders and nobles who lived in Naboth's city with him. In those letters she wrote:

"Proclaim a day of fasting and seat Naboth in a prominent place among the people. But seat two scoundrels opposite him and have them bring charges that he has cursed both God and the king. Then take him out and stone him to death."

So the elders and nobles who lived in Naboth's city did as Jezebel directed in the letters she had written to them. They proclaimed a fast and seated Naboth in a prominent place among the people. Then two scoundrels came and sat opposite him and brought charges against Naboth before the people, saying, "Naboth has cursed both God and the king." So they took him outside the city and stoned him to death. Then they sent word to Jezebel: "Naboth has been stoned to death."

As soon as Jezebel heard that Naboth had been stoned to death, she said to Ahab, "Get up and take possession of the vineyard of Naboth the Jezreelite that he refused to sell you. He is no longer alive, but dead." When Ahab heard that Naboth was dead, he got up and went down to take possession of Naboth's vineyard.

Then the word of the LORD came to Elijah the Tishbite: "Go down to meet Ahab king of Israel, who rules in Samaria. He is now in Naboth's vineyard, where he has gone to take possession of it. Say to him, 'This is what the LORD says: Have you not murdered a man and seized his property?' Then say to him, 'This is what the LORD says: In the place where dogs licked up Naboth's blood, dogs will lick up your blood—yes, yours!'"

1 Kings 21:25

> There was never anyone like Ahab, who sold him-
> self to do evil in the eyes of the LORD, urged on by
> Jezebel his wife.

Hebrews 10:24–25

> And let us consider how we may spur one another
> on toward love and good deeds, not giving up
> meeting together, as some are in the habit of doing,
> but encouraging one another—and all the more as
> you see the Day approaching.

FOR YOUR CONSIDERATION

History has been shaped, positively and negatively, by powerful couples of influence, like Franklin and Eleanor Roosevelt, John F. and Jackie Kennedy, and Winston and Clementine Churchill. And there are famous couples (infamous more like) who went rogue, like Bonnie and Clyde, who crossed America in a spree of robbery and murder.

But influence is not just given to the powerful and famous. Every one of us has influence, in different ways. At the grocery-store checkout, in a casual interaction with a neighbor or a work colleague, we influence and make an impact either for good or for ill.

Pastor J. R. Miller said:

> There have been meetings of only a moment which
> have left impressions for life, for eternity. No one
> of us can understand that mysterious thing we call
> influence ... yet out of every one of us continually
> virtue goes, either to heal, to bless, to leave marks
> of beauty; or to wound, to hurt, to poison, to stain
> other lives.[1]

As we turn to a pair of infamous biblical villains, we encounter a pair of true, tragic partners in crime. The dangerous partnership of King Ahab and Queen Jezebel was the result of a much larger, darker alliance—a peace treaty made by Ahab's father, Omri. Linking arms with the powerful Phoenician nation made complete sense to King Omri, because both Israel and Phoenicia were under threat from Syria. And young Princess Jezebel was given to Prince Ahab to seal the deal. This was a political union.

Jezebel was no stranger to death: her own father ruled in Tyre because he had assumed the role of political assassin. According to the Jewish historian Josephus, Jezebel's father had been a longtime priest of Astarte who had murdered his brother, King Philetes, ascending to the throne at the age of thirty-six.

The law specifically prohibited God's people from marrying foreign wives, not because of racism, but because of the tendency for them to be corrupted by false religion. And that is exactly how things played out with Ahab: his love for his wife soon led him to build a temple in Samaria, dedicated to Baal worship. Scripture tells us he was "urged on" by his wife. Our friendships and partnerships profoundly affect our behavior. Are ours healthy?

Jezebel was the sworn enemy of the mighty Elijah, whom God raised up to bring the nation to repentance. And so she used her influence to try to manipulate him, intimidating and threatening him. And it worked—the man who had called down fire from heaven ran for his life, terrified.

Upset by Elijah's prophetic ministry, and the judgment of drought that he commanded, Jezebel sent him a death threat. Commentators have criticized Elijah for running, but she was the most formidable power in the land and was systematically persecuting and killing the prophets of God in her zeal for Baal worship. Jezebel's method was designed to create terror too. She could have sent an assassin; instead, she sent a messenger who announced an assassination to come. The queen didn't need to use a hired killer when a threat would suffice. And then she used a chilling image to drive the threat home, as she would have a self-imprecatory oath, running a finger across her throat as she vowed that Elijah would be as dead and bloodied as those prophets of Baal that had been slain on the slopes of Mount Carmel. She used threats to get her way, and almost succeeded.

She was also a master of subtlety and political maneuvering in her manipulation. She set out to frame Naboth, an innocent, good man, because she wanted her husband to complete a land deal. Jezebel was the driving force behind the blatant injustice that followed.

Naboth was obeying the law of God:

> No inheritance in Israel is to pass from one tribe to another, for every Israelite shall keep the tribal inheritance of their ancestors. (Num. 36:7)

But Jezebel, staggered by what she viewed as her husband's weak behavior, executed a cunning plan to shine a spotlight of false recognition upon Naboth, only to then accuse him of treason—a capital offense, which led to him being stoned to death.

This was the trigger that ushered in judgment on both Ahab and Jezebel, even though there was a brief temporary reprieve for Ahab because he responded with repentance. But although his crime was murder and covetousness, note that the crime of injustice against the poor was the last straw. Everybody has the ability to be manipulative, to be hateful and deceitful.

When it came time for her death, it seems that Jezebel still tried to use her influence to manipulate. Teacher Janet Howe Gaines wrote:

> When Jezebel herself finally appears again in the pages of the Bible, it is for her death scene. Jehu, with the blood of Joram still on his hands, races his chariot into Jezreel to continue the insurrection by assassinating Jezebel.... Realizing that Jehu is on his way to kill her, Jezebel does not disguise herself and flee the city, as a more cowardly person might do. Instead, she calmly prepares for his arrival by performing three acts: "She painted her eyes with kohl and dressed her hair, and she looked out of the window" (2 Kings 9:30). The traditional interpretation is that Jezebel primps and coquettishly looks out the window in an effort to seduce Jehu, that she wishes to win his favor and become part of his

harem in order to save her own life, such treachery indicating Jezebel's dastardly betrayal of deceased family members. According to this reading, Jezebel sheds familial loyalty as easily as a snake sheds its skin in an attempt to ensure her continued pleasure and safety at court.

Applying eye makeup (kohl) and brushing one's hair are often connected to flirting in Hebraic thinking. Isaiah 3:16, Jeremiah 4:30, Ezekiel 23:40 and Proverbs 6:24–26 provide examples of women who bat their painted eyes to lure innocent men into adulterous beds. Black kohl is widely incorporated in Bible passages as a symbol of feminine deception and trickery, and its use to paint the area above and below the eyelids is generally considered part of a woman's arsenal of artifice. In Jezebel's case, however, the cosmetic is more than just an attempt to accentuate the eyes. Jezebel is donning the female version of armor as she prepares to do battle.[2]

She went to her death with a sarcastic tongue, calling Jehu "Zimri"—the name of a usurper king who reigned for only seven days.

Jezebel's name was probably originally "Jeze-bul," a name that means "where is Prince Baal?"—a terrible and fitting name for someone who was so familiar with the hideous ceremonies used to call upon Baal for his help.

But she underwent an unsubtle name change, probably at the hands of Elijah. "Jeze-bel" means "where is the dung?" When Elijah challenged her prophets on Mount Carmel, he engaged in some crude humor, asking if Baal was going to the bathroom—a fact somewhat lost in the sanitized translations of the Scriptures.

And after her violent death, worse things happened to her name. In the New Testament, her name is used symbolically to refer to someone who is seducing the congregation at Thyatira to practice fornication and eat food sacrificed to idols (Rev. 2:20). Forever her name is associated with death, seduction, and pride; one writer said that she was "proud of her pride." What a terrible legacy. What will we leave behind us? To be sure, we will all leave a legacy, for good or ill. Let's choose well, and be an influence for good and for God.

Jezebel "urged" Ahab on to evil; in contrast, we are instructed in the New Testament to carefully consider how we can "spur" each other on toward love and good deeds. This is active, intentional work that we're called to; the word "spur" is usually used in the New Testament to describe discomfort (like a horse would feel if the rider used spurs!). Mutual encouragement doesn't just happen. As we think about and pray for others, we can thoughtfully consider ways to bless them.

If you are using the DVD, watch session 6.

STUDY AND DISCUSSION

1. Have you ever experienced manipulation? What was the method, and the effect, of it?

2. In thinking about the legacy that we leave, what one word would you like to be associated with your name after you've passed?

3. What are some ways that we might encourage and "spur each other on"?

GOING DEEPER

"Half of the people lie with their lips; the other half with their tears," wrote essayist Nassim Nicholas Taleb. As we think about manipulation, what does this mean?

THIS SESSION'S CHALLENGE

Identify someone in your life, and prayerfully consider how you might encourage and bless that person.

DAILY BIBLE NOTES: JEZEBEL
Day 1. Urged On

Read: 1 Kings 21:25–26; Hebrews 10:24–25

Focus: "There was never anyone like Ahab, who sold himself to do evil in the eyes of the LORD, urged on by Jezebel his wife" (1 Kings 21:25).

I was intrigued by how quickly the conversation went downhill. Enjoying a fun dinner with friends, someone shared a story that was a little off-color. Without sounding prudish, the nervous glances around the table confirmed that we all felt that a line had been crossed. But within minutes, caution was thrown to the wind, and people were telling jokes and using words that were uncommon in our group. I wondered, what just happened? It all began by someone giving permission, and their action urged others to jump in and join in too. We can all live permissively, or provocatively, offering those around us a license to sin, or we can live beautifully and so encouraging goodness. We create a culture around us by our own behavior, good or bad. To put it somewhat bluntly in Bible terms, either we can "spur one another on toward love and good deeds" or we can act like Jezebel, who "urged" her husband toward evil. Today, I'd like to be a positive example. How about you?

Pray: May I be an influence for You, for purity, for goodness, for love, this day, loving Father. Amen.

Day 2. True Success in the Eyes of God

Read: 1 Kings 22:39; 16:30–33

Focus: "As for the other events of Ahab's reign, including all he did, the palace he built and adorned with ivory, and the cities he fortified, are they not written in the book of the annals of the kings of Israel?" (1 Kings 22:39).

He was highly successful as a politician, making trade deals that boosted the economy. After years of war, he oversaw two decades of peace. He boosted the defense budget for his nation, building a huge army. He built cities. His wife was sophisticated, coming from a culture of poets and writers—her nation gave the world the alphabet. And he was rich, with an opulent house crammed with luxury goods. We know he built a palace adorned with ivory; although there's some speculation about the integrity of the find, archaeologists have uncovered the remains of a home in the area where he lived. Every wall was breathtaking, paneled from floor to ceiling with intricately carved ivory; figures of lions, griffins, and sphinxes stared down. The place overflowed with the trappings of royalty. Even the bed ends, tabletops, and chair backs were ivory-clad.

And for all this, Ahab was judged as being one of the worst kings in Israel's entire history, a man who deeply angered the Lord.

It's a theme that we'll return to later, but one that's worth underlining: true success in the eyes of God is not measured in terms of financial gain, business acumen, or fame. The suave and sophisticated don't impress Him. Rather, it's integrity and faithfulness that catch His eye and warm His heart.

As we'll see in tomorrow's Bible notes, Ahab did some good things. But he was inconsistent and too easily swayed by the occultic obsessions of his wife, Jezebel, who was a passionate advocate of all things to do with Baal.

Let's pursue true success.

Pray: May my life reflect Your values, Lord, rather than superficial values of success. Amen.

Day 3. Jezebel's Husband, Ahab: Moral Weakling

Read: 1 Kings 16:29–34; Romans 12:1–2

Focus: "He set up an altar for Baal in the temple of Baal that he built in Samaria" (1 Kings 16:32).

In the Walt Disney cartoon film *Robin Hood*, the evil Prince John is portrayed as a skinny lion who shouts and screams and wields absolute power, but sticks his thumb in his mouth and goes into a tantrum whenever life gets difficult. Ahab was such a character—one of those moody types who would sulk like a child when he didn't get his way.

He did some good things, though. He led Israel into victory against her enemies. He listened to prophets and went through times of repentance. But he was also a moral weakling, a man who lacked conviction and decisiveness. He didn't even share his bride's single-minded commitment to the Baals. In fact, it would seem that Ahab was incapable of being single minded about anything. Ever the man to please, Ahab had himself set up a special sacred stone monument to the Baals near to the altar of the occultic temple, and just to be on the safe side, he threw in a pole in honor of goddess Asherah for good measure.

He even named three of his children in honor of Yahweh: Jehoram ("Yahweh is high"), Ahaziah ("Yahweh has taken hold"), and Athaliah ("Yahweh is exalted"). Ahab was a man of religious tokenism, willing to treat the God of heaven and the devil of hell like good-luck charms, to use and discard at will.

And he goes down in history as a man who heard what God wanted, but wavered constantly and didn't obey.

Sometimes it's difficult to stand firm and strong in the midst of the pressures of our culture. But let's do it.

Pray: Establish me firmly in You, Lord, confident in who You are, and confident in who I am in You. Amen.

Day 4. Jezebel: A Hardened Heart

Read: 1 Kings 18:1–4; 19:1–2

Focus: "While Jezebel was killing off the LORD's prophets, Obadiah had taken a hundred prophets and hidden them in two caves, fifty in each, and had supplied them with food and water" (1 Kings 18:4).

Over forty years of ministry, I've witnessed wonderful examples of transformation and growth in people's lives as they've walked with Jesus. Who they are today bears no resemblance to who they were, and they have allowed God to do wonders in and through them. And I've also seen others for whom the opposite is true. Allowing patterns of sinful behavior to become established, they have walked a downhill pathway, slowly, gradually getting deeper into darkness. Just today I heard of a minister friend (and fellow student when I was in Bible college) who has ruined his life, marriage, and ministry because of a destructive secret lifestyle.

When Jezebel challenged Elijah and dispatched a messenger with a bloodthirsty threat, this was not the first time she had sinned in this way; she had already been engaged in a campaign of murder against the prophets of the Lord. That's one reason for Elijah's fear: he knew full well that she was more than capable of carrying out her death threat.

When God convicts, let's be quick to respond, and not harden our hearts. He convicts because He loves, and wants to spare us pain.

Pray: May my heart always be both tender and responsive to Your call, Father. Amen.

Day 5. Ahab's and Jezebel's Endings

Read: 1 Kings 21:1–29; 2 Kings 9:30–37

Focus: "In the place where dogs licked up Naboth's blood, dogs will lick up your blood—yes, yours!" (1 Kings 21:19).

The Bible is an amazing book. Clear and detailed predictive prophecy is repeatedly fulfilled, sometimes with gaps of hundreds or thousands of years between the prediction and the fulfillment. So it was with Jezebel and Ahab. Despite disguising himself to go into battle, a stray arrow found its way in a chink in Ahab's armor, and he died. Elijah had prophesied that dogs would lick up Ahab's blood, which came true, although the judgment that his body would be left in Naboth's vineyard was deferred to his son, Joram, again, exactly as God had decreed (1 Kings 21:29; 2 Kings 9:25). And then the similar judgment in Jezebel came about, perhaps ten years after her husband's death. Despite seeing what happened to him, Jezebel made no attempt to repent and continued to exercise influence during the reigns of her two sons Ahaziah and Jehoram, and in the southern kingdom, Judah, where her daughter Athaliah became queen (2 Kings 8:18).

But she could not escape judgment, and at last, at the command of Jehu, she was thrown from a window. And the dogs came by. The word of the Lord was once again fulfilled.

Even through this rather horrifying story, we see that the Bible is not just a storybook, but the reliable account of a God who intervenes powerfully in history. His Word stands forever.

Pray: Your Word is true, and You span the years, mighty God. I worship You. Amen.

Day 6. Catch Me If You Can

Read: 2 Kings 9:30–37; Galatians 6:1–10

Frank Abagnale is a man who had an unusual ability to wangle his way out of tricky situations. Gifted with criminal ingenuity, he successfully posed as a pilot, a doctor, and a prosecutor. So colorful is his story that it inspired a film starring Leonardo DiCaprio and Tom Hanks. Abagnale conned millions of dollars by becoming an expert in check fraud. His life shows that there are some people who are able to turn adversity into profit by making shrewd moves. Before we leave the horrible episode where Jezebel meets her end, it's worth noting that some speculate that she adjusted her makeup and hair because she thought she might be able to seduce Jehu and so be spared. We've seen that she had shown great cunning in her life, setting Elijah on the run, and single handedly creating the conspiracy that led to her husband getting control of Naboth's vineyard. Now, perhaps she could use her skills on Jehu. She never learned.

Sooner of later, most of us come to the conclusion that we need help in life, that we don't have the ability to come out of every situation as winners. Frank Abagnale now earns millions of dollars training companies about check fraud. But Jezebel didn't fare so well.

Ponder: Is there a life lesson that we really need to embrace?

JUDAS ISCARIOT
The Call to Surrender

CONNECTING WITH ONE ANOTHER

If you go on vacation with family or friends, do you become "managerial" about what you do each day? Or do you assume a passive role? How does it normally work out?

KEY THOUGHT THIS SESSION

Playwright Bernard Shaw said, "God made man in his own image—unfortunately man has returned the favor." We can all be guilty of wanting God to be what we want Him to be—and perhaps this was a key part of Judas' downfall: he tried to manage God. We, too, can be guilty of attempting the same thing.

SCRIPTURE TO READ

Matthew 26:14–16

Then one of the Twelve—the one called Judas Iscariot—went to the chief priests and asked, "What are you willing to give me if I deliver him over to you?" So they counted out for him thirty pieces of silver. From then on Judas watched for an opportunity to hand him over.

Matthew 16:21–23

From that time on Jesus began to explain to his disciples that he must go to Jerusalem and suffer many things at the hands of the elders, the chief priests and the teachers of the law, and that he must be killed and on the third day be raised to life.

Peter took him aside and began to rebuke him. "Never, Lord!" he said. "This shall never happen to you!"

Jesus turned and said to Peter, "Get behind me, Satan! You are a stumbling block to me; you do not have in mind the concerns of God, but merely human concerns."

Matthew 27:3–5

When Judas, who had betrayed him, saw that Jesus was condemned, he was seized with remorse and returned the thirty pieces of silver to the chief priests and the elders. "I have sinned," he said, "for I have betrayed innocent blood."

"What is that to us?" they replied. "That's your responsibility."

So Judas threw the money into the temple and left. Then he went away and hanged himself.

Acts 1:18–19

With the payment he received for his wickedness, Judas bought a field; there he fell headlong, his body burst open and all his intestines spilled out. Everyone in Jerusalem heard about this, so they called that field in their language Akeldama, that is, Field of Blood.

FOR YOUR CONSIDERATION

Jesus had to deal with many challenges as His ministry unfolded. His disciples misunderstood what He taught them and needed constant clarification. His own people in Nazareth, where He was raised, rejected Him, forcing Him to transfer His base of operations to Capernaum. The Pharisees set traps for Him, accused Him, and waged a campaign to undermine and ultimately kill Him.

But one of the more subtle challenges was that people repeatedly tried to manage Him. The disciples wanted to send parents and children away; Peter didn't want Jesus to go to the cross; and Martha and Mary were upset when He didn't immediately go to help Lazarus.

And then there was Judas Iscariot. Surely the most well-known traitor in history, Judas is repeatedly referred to in the Gospels as "the one who betrayed Jesus" (see Matt. 10:4; Mark 3:19; Luke 6:16). Despite spending three years as a member of Jesus' team, Judas is remembered simply as a traitor; it's the headline over his life. But just why did he do it? What was his motive?

Judas appeared faithful. When others, like Peter, doubted the wisdom of Jesus' going to the cross, there's no record of Judas protesting. Peter initially refused to allow Jesus to wash his feet, but Judas acquiesced without hesitation.

Perhaps management was Judas' problem. Remember that the Jews wanted a military Messiah, one who would deliver them from the oppression of the Romans. Living under the heel of another nation, where the occupiers were exacting heavy tax burdens and harsh controls, the people of Israel longed for a human rescuer. When Salome, the mother of James and John, heard that Jesus was heading for Jerusalem, she went to Jesus and asked for thrones for her boys: she thought this was the moment for the long-awaited take-over. And the idea lingered even after the resurrection, because the early believers were still asking, "Lord, are you at this time going to restore the kingdom to Israel?" (Acts 1:6). I firmly believe that

Judas so wanted Jesus to take that political route, and betrayed Him because He was headed to a cross instead.

Matthew tells us exactly when Judas decided to finally go through with his betrayal scheme: it was after Jesus was anointed for burial. At this stage, Judas knew for sure that triumph over the Romans in Jerusalem was not going to happen—Jesus was determined to head toward death. And instead of rebuking the occupiers, Jesus was concentrating on rebuking some of His own people, the Jews, like the Pharisees, and the money changers in the Temple courts. So some think that, with the smell of burial spices in his nostrils, Judas set up the betrayal in the hope that this would force a showdown, and edge Jesus into the role of a military Messiah. When we consider that Peter drew his sword and chopped off a hapless chap's ear as the beginning of a fight, we can see that Judas might not have been the only disciple with a confrontational plan.

Judas shows us that we can not only try to manage God but get upset when we can't force Him to do what we want. Resentment drives trust out of our hearts. Let's be careful when our repeated prayers seem to go unanswered, or when God seems set on pursuing a direction that we don't like. He is God, and although the invitation to prayer means He is open to suggestions, ultimately He decides. Let's allow the challenge to come to us: "Where am I trying to manage God?" Let God be God. It's a call that we all need to heed.

We, too, then, are in danger—in danger of misunderstanding Jesus and of being seduced by our own dreams and visions for life. In doing this work, we betray Jesus. Paul was brutally honest with the threat of this possibility. He warned about those who might "follow Satan" (1 Tim. 5:15) and who might be snared by the devil "to do his will"

(2 Tim. 2:26). John's own pastoral experience made him face Christians who knew the faith well but corrupted it and stood against Christ. He named such people "antichrists" (1 John 2:18, 22; 4:3; 2 John 1:7).

Judas shows us that generally people don't fall into sin—they slide, and there are key turning points along the way when bad decisions are made. Judas made a wrong turn somewhere and courageously pressed ahead instead of admitting his mistake, going back, and retracing his steps. Before long he was in the realm of darkness. In John 13:11, Jesus knew this and called him "unclean." Then, ever so gradually, Judas became a pawn of the evil one. It is frightening to watch Judas run out into the "night," where people stumble; this is where the light is despised.

Are we currently at a place where we are making poor choices, ignoring the consequences? Is this a moment to repent and choose well rather than pressing on toward disaster?

Judas is also a portrait of the battle that we are involved in: spiritual warfare is a reality.

In the great struggle between light and darkness, between truth and falsehood, between God and Satan, Judas became a vessel of God's opponents. While the actual "handing over" of Jesus occurs in John 18, the critical moment in Judas' life takes place in 13:27: "As soon as Judas took the bread, Satan entered into him." From this juncture, Judas is barely his own person. He has been absorbed by darkness. The last image we have is of a man filled with regret, who tries to return his payment for the betrayal. But it is refused, and Judas commits suicide (Matt. 27:1–10; Acts 1:16–20).

If you are using the DVD, watch session 7.

STUDY AND DISCUSSION

1. What does "surrendering to God" involve?

2. How do we make surrender a daily choice?

3. "People don't fall into sin—they slide." Do you agree with this statement? Are there areas of your life where appropriate sharing and prayer might be needed?

GOING DEEPER

Sociologist Émile Durkheim said, "Every tribe/society invents a god who reflects its values, standards, aspirations, hopes, ambitions and attitudes and then worships it—thus legitimating its own standards of behavior." How might that happen with sin in our culture?

THIS SESSION'S CHALLENGE

Ask the Lord to show you a new aspect of His character, and also to show you where you might be trying to "manage" Him.

DAILY BIBLE NOTES: JUDAS ISCARIOT
Day 1. The Great Pretender

Read: Luke 22:7–23; Matthew 23:23–36

Focus: "They began to question among themselves which of them it might be who would do this" (Luke 22:23).

Recently I read a rather enjoyable but disturbing book about a man who infiltrated a conservative Christian university in the US. An atheist, he posed as a committed believer so that he could get the inside scoop on the thinking and practices of the other students. Apparently he did rather well as an impostor: nobody suspected, and he looked and sounded like an authentic follower of Jesus.

Among the many dark statements that the New Testament makes about Judas, we know that he had his hand in the till, stealing money from the disciples' collective purse, and we obviously know that he betrayed Jesus, again, with money involved. That doesn't mean he was always bad; after all, people don't fall—they slide. However, there was a pattern of dishonesty that developed. And notice that the other disciples had no suspicion that Judas was not a fully committed member of the team. Jesus knew, and referred to His betrayer by offering him bread and wine first at the Last Supper, but the rest of the Twelve had no clue and began nervously speculating about the identity of the traitor. Judas fitted right in. He gave no clues about his true motives or actions.

As a reader of daily Bible notes, it's unlikely that you're deliberately pretending to be a Christian. But we can all play less obvious spiritual games of cover-up, as we consistently sin and sweep away our tracks. If faith is more about performance than authentic commitment, it's time to get real.

Pray: Lord, enable me to live authentically today. Amen.

Day 2. Prompted by Satan

Read: John 13:2, 27; Acts 5:1–3

Focus: "The evening meal was in progress, and the devil had already prompted Judas, the son of Simon Iscariot, to betray Jesus" (John 13:2).

It was a phrase that is sometimes used when Christians make a terrible choice and fall into serious sin: "The devil made me do it." The implication is that we are not really responsible for our failures, but are hapless before the enemy who is the tempter. We are not to blame, we think and say—Satan is. But the Bible offers us no room to excuse our follies like this. There is a dark personality, one who consistently and cunningly pursues a mission to undermine God's purposes and distract and tempt God's people—we need to affirm that truth in a culture that often mocks the idea of evil and dark powers. But the devil can't make anyone do anything. John reiterates the devil's activities in Judas' heart and life, and even goes so far as to identify the devil as the one who prompted the betrayal. But there's never any suggestion that Judas wasn't fully responsible for his own actions. He chose freely.

Sin creates deception, and self-deception is the ultimate blindness. Caught in sin, we can rationalize, squirm, insist that we are right, that everyone else is doing what we've done—and we can point a finger of blame at the enemy. But while Satan can prompt, we are the ones who respond to the prompting. Perhaps we're feeling a nudge to go in what we know is the wrong direction. Don't fall for it. And if we've already succumbed to the nudge, let's turn around and take responsibility. We choose. So, God helping us, let's choose well.

Pray: When Satan whispers, help me to see and hear clearly, and act responsibly. Amen.

Day 3. Trusted by Jesus

Read: John 12:1–6; Matthew 28:16–20

Focus: "He did not say this because he cared about the poor but because he was a thief; as keeper of the money bag, he used to help himself to what was put into it" (John 12:6).

We Christians are often told, rightly, that we need to trust God. It's a message that needs to be reiterated. Faith is frequently celebrated, but we should honor faithfulness and trust too. If you're trusting God through difficult times right now, hanging on even though you have many unanswered questions, may you be encouraged as you trust.

But let's see, too, that God trusts us. When Jesus ascended to heaven after the resurrection, He entrusted the most important message in history—the good news of the gospel—to His rather unpredictable and fragile disciples. The initial spokesperson for the initiative was the impetuous Peter, known for his fireside betrayal of Christ. But not only were they called to believe in Jesus, but He believed in them—and He believes in us.

We've already seen that Judas had been appointed as the treasurer for Jesus' team, a decision that was no doubt approved of by Jesus. He was crooked, and was pilfering the funds, which was why he was incensed when Mary used perfume worth an enormous amount—the equivalent of a year's income for the average person—and anointed Jesus with it. Judas protested about waste, and made a pious speech about poverty, which the other disciples had sympathy with. But lurking beneath the high-sounding words was greed. Judas had betrayed Jesus' trust before he ever met with the religious authorities or proffered a kiss in Gethsemane. Jesus trusts us. Let's not let Him down.

Pray: Lord, I believe in You. Help me to believe that, wonderfully, You believe in me. Amen.

Day 4. Accuser and Defender

Read: John 12:1–8; 19:1–30

Focus: "'Leave her alone,' Jesus replied. 'It was intended that she should save this perfume for the day of my burial'" (John 12:7).

In this episode when Jesus was anointed with perfume, notice the beautiful way in which He defended Mary after Judas accused her of wastefulness. The victim of the muttered sniping of the disciples in general and Judas in particular, she must have felt embarrassed and shamed. But Jesus stepped in and rebuked her critics.

Later, Jesus would promise His disciples that another comforter was coming—in other words, one just like Him—because He was going away in the resurrection and ascension. The Holy Spirit is the Paraclete, the One who comes alongside. "Comforter" is a word that makes God sound like a quilt, or one who commiserates at a funeral. But the word really means "advocate," one who comes along to defend in legal proceedings. Jesus defended, and the Holy Spirit continues that work.

Perhaps you see God more as the accuser than the defender, and of course, as we've seen, there will be times when the Holy Spirit convicts. But there is also another accuser: Satan. In the Old Testament, a "satan" could be a human enemy, while the Holy Spirit is the One who gives us assurance when memories of old errors and sins surface.

Some people see God only as a judge. But the person of Christ and the work of the Holy Spirit show us that He is also the defender of His people. Does Satan accuse? By faith, stand behind Jesus. He is the One who has paid for our guilt and shame in full. He cried, "It is finished." Let Him and His great work be our sole defense.

Pray: You alone are my reason for confidence in the face of my regrets and shame, Lord. Thank You for being my Lord, my rock, my defender. Amen.

Day 5. Still a Friend

Read: Matthew 26:47–56; Mark 14:43–50

Focus: "Jesus replied, 'Do what you came for, friend'" (Matt. 26:50).

It's an old, beautiful hymn that has brought comfort to so many, especially in tougher seasons of life: what a friend we have in Jesus. And I have certainly found Him to be the best friend; faithful when I have been faithless, blessing me in ways that I never imagined possible, and forgiving me when I fail. We see that faithfulness in the way Jesus responded to Judas. He washed the feet of His betrayer in the upper room during that poignant last supper. Then, when

Judas summitted the height of hypocrisy with a kiss, a gesture usually reserved for the closest of companions, Jesus addressed him as friend. There's not a hint of sarcasm here, and as Jesus said, "Do what you came for," some commentators suggest that He was actually asking Judas if he really wanted to go through with his treacherous plan. But the kiss was an identifying sign, showing those with Judas whom they needed to arrest.

As I write this today, I sit in the grounds of the Holocaust museum in Jerusalem. Grainy photographs and old film footage give disturbing testimony to the truth that sin is dark. We human beings are capable of monstrous acts. And sin is not just about the extremes, like the genocide of the Holocaust. It's expressed in our everyday acts of rebellion, bitterness, and hatred; humanity is deeply flawed. But there is a friend who sticks closer than a brother, and His graciousness towers over our sinfulness: His name is Jesus. All His friends abandoned Him. But He never abandons us. Today, let's be grateful—and faithful.

Pray: You are the greatest friend I could possibly have, Lord. Walk close today. Amen.

Day 6. A Horrible End

Read: Matthew 27:3–5; Acts 1:16–20

There's no getting away from the horror that is the end of Judas' story, as he returned the blood money that he had been given as a fee for his betrayal and then ended his life. I think it's superficial to believe that he did this for money alone; although, as we've already seen, greed was one of his vices.

But today, let's see that sin is not on level ground; when we embark on a pattern of habitual sin, refusing to acknowledge it and repent, we begin a downhill slide. Perhaps Judas began by "borrowing" some money from the shared financial pot. Then he started adjusting the team accounts in his own favor. Then larger sums of money were taken. Deflecting the guilt that he felt as a thief, he became critical of others, like the woman who brought that extravagant gift of perfume. Before long, he was walking swiftly toward full-on betrayal. Let me make the point one more time: people don't fall—they slide. Judas' story serves as a sad lesson. Let's learn well.

Ponder: Am I on a downhill trajectory in any area of my life?

HEROD "THE GREAT"

The Call to True Greatness

CONNECTING WITH ONE ANOTHER

Who is the greatest human being you have ever known, and why?

KEY THOUGHT THIS SESSION

In a world where people seem thirsty for fame, Jesus redefines what true greatness is. And Herod, a man who has been tagged as "great" throughout history, was anything but great.

SCRIPTURE TO READ

Matthew 2:1–23

> After Jesus was born in Bethlehem in Judea, during
> the time of King Herod, Magi from the east came

to Jerusalem and asked, "Where is the one who has been born king of the Jews? We saw his star when it rose and have come to worship him."

When King Herod heard this he was disturbed, and all Jerusalem with him. When he had called together all the people's chief priests and teachers of the law, he asked them where the Messiah was to be born. "In Bethlehem in Judea," they replied, "for this is what the prophet has written:

"'But you, Bethlehem, in the land of Judah,
    are by no means least among the rulers of
        Judah;
for out of you will come a ruler
    who will shepherd my people Israel.'"

Then Herod called the Magi secretly and found out from them the exact time the star had appeared. He sent them to Bethlehem and said, "Go and search carefully for the child. As soon as you find him, report to me, so that I too may go and worship him."

After they had heard the king, they went on their way, and the star they had seen when it rose went ahead of them until it stopped over the place where the child was. When they saw the star, they were overjoyed. On coming to the house, they saw the child with his mother Mary, and they bowed down and worshiped him. Then they opened their treasures and presented him with gifts of gold, frankincense and myrrh. And having been warned in a dream not to go back to Herod, they returned to their country by another route.

When they had gone, an angel of the Lord appeared to Joseph in a dream. "Get up," he said, "take the child and his mother and escape to Egypt. Stay there until I tell you, for Herod is going to search for the child to kill him."

So he got up, took the child and his mother during the night and left for Egypt, where he stayed until the death of Herod. And so was fulfilled what the Lord had said through the prophet: "Out of Egypt I called my son."

When Herod realized that he had been outwitted by the Magi, he was furious, and he gave orders to kill all the boys in Bethlehem and its vicinity who were two years old and under, in accordance with the time he had learned from the Magi. Then what was said through the prophet Jeremiah was fulfilled:

"A voice is heard in Ramah,
　　weeping and great mourning,
Rachel weeping for her children
　　and refusing to be comforted,
　　because they are no more."

After Herod died, an angel of the Lord appeared in a dream to Joseph in Egypt and said, "Get up, take the child and his mother and go to the land of Israel, for those who were trying to take the child's life are dead."

So he got up, took the child and his mother and went to the land of Israel. But when he heard that Archelaus was reigning in Judea in place of his father Herod, he was afraid to go there. Having been warned in a dream, he withdrew to the district of Galilee, and he went and lived in a town called Nazareth. So was fulfilled what was said through the prophets, that he would be called a Nazarene.

Matthew 20:20–28

Then the mother of Zebedee's sons came to Jesus with her sons and, kneeling down, asked a favor of him.

"What is it you want?" he asked.

She said, "Grant that one of these two sons of mine may sit at your right and the other at your left in your kingdom."

"You don't know what you are asking," Jesus said to them. "Can you drink the cup I am going to drink?"

"We can," they answered.

Jesus said to them, "You will indeed drink from my cup, but to sit at my right or left is not for me to grant. These places belong to those for whom they have been prepared by my Father."

When the ten heard about this, they were indignant with the two brothers. Jesus called them together and said, "You know that the rulers of the Gentiles lord it over them, and their high officials exercise authority over them. Not so with you. Instead, whoever wants to become great among you must be your servant, and whoever wants to be first must be your slave—just as the Son of Man did not come to be served, but to serve, and to give his life as a ransom for many."

Mark 9:33–34

They came to Capernaum. When he was in the house, he asked them, "What were you arguing about on the road?" But they kept quiet because on the way they had argued about who was the greatest.

FOR YOUR CONSIDERATION

It's often called "the most wonderful time of the year." At Christmastime, everything looks more beautiful in the soft hues of the Christmas tree lights, and the flickering candles in church. It's all very warm, the season of cheer, peace on earth, goodwill to all humans. But there's an aspect of Christmas that we tend to overlook: the murderous reach of a dark tyrant called Herod the Great. The instigator of a campaign of infanticide in Bethlehem, Herod is the often ignored villain of the Christmas story.

So why is he called "Great"? His achievements were many. Greatness is often defined by power, fame, and wealth, and Herod checked all of those boxes. A shrewd politician, he was also great as a soldier, an orator, and a builder. He rose to power as a young man, initially ruling Galilee as governor at the age of twenty-five, later to become king of Judaea. And he was an astute politician who managed to stay in favor with various Roman administrations.

During his thirty-three years of rule, he built ports and palaces, and fortresses like Masada. A sponsor of the Olympic Games, he patronized art and sport.

One of his more impressive achievements was the building of the Temple. It was a spectacular sight, and if the list of the wonders of the world had not been closed out, Herod's temple in Jerusalem would surely have been added to it. Desperate to curry favor from his own people, and wanting to make amends for his cruel persecution of some members of the rabbinic community, Herod set about to rebuild the Temple—and it was a mammoth project. It took ten thousand men ten years just to build the retaining walls (one of which, the Western, or Wailing, Wall, still stands today). The grounds were part of a plateau that could house twenty-four football fields, a gathering place for the six to seven million Jews who lived in the Roman Empire and who would make regular pilgrimages to Jerusalem to attend the various feasts and festivals.

The Jews had a saying: "He who has not seen Herod's building has never in his life seen a truly grand building." The Temple was noted for its magnificence at the time of Jesus (see Mark 13:1). But there was one aspect to the amazing temple that the Jews hated: Herod had placed a huge Roman eagle at the main entrance, a symbol that was sacrilegious to the Jews. Herod wanted to be popular religiously and politically. Faith makes a poor partner with the state. Being a good Christian is not the same as being a compliant citizen: sometimes we have to make a stand against the popular view, rather than go with the flow, a point that we will see more clearly in the final session of this book.

Herod was deeply distrusted by his fellow Jews, who viewed him as a Roman lackey and an agent of oppressive taxation. He failed with his family and was plagued by problems with his ten wives and his children. He ordered the execution of his Hasmonean wife, Mariamne, of their two sons, Alexander and Aristobulus, of other members of the Hasmonean family, and of his son Antipater. He left a legacy of strife: after his death in 4 BC, Augustus Caesar resolved the dispute that broke out among three of Herod's surviving sons by dividing the kingdom but withholding the royal title of "king" from all of the heirs.

And despite his power, he was deeply insecure, which was one reason why he was so disturbed and angry about the birth of the real King of Kings, Jesus. The Bethlehem massacre reflects Herod's influence and jealousy. His attempt to discover the rival King of the Jews resulted in the murder of several innocent children. Herod's building programs were fueled by paranoia, so terrified was he that he would lose his kingdom. He accused his sons of treason and had them killed simply because he felt threatened by them. It's recorded that:

> He also sent his sons to Sebaste, a city not far from
> Caesarea, and ordered them to be there strangled ...
> And this was the end of Alexander and Aristobulus.[1]

He was so concerned that his favorite wife, Mariamne, might end up in the arms of another that he instructed his soldiers to kill her if anything were to happen to him while traveling abroad. Eventually he killed her parents, and then he had her tried and executed too.

SO WHAT IS TRUE GREATNESS?

"I am the greatest," boasted Cassius Clay, the boxer who became Muhammad Ali. John Lennon once boasted that the Beatles had become more famous than Jesus.

Even Jesus' disciples jostled for power and argued about who was the greatest among them; and Salome, the mother of James and John, requested royal thrones for her sons. But Jesus redefined greatness, showing it to have little to do with wealth, fame, or power, but rather with humility and self-forgetting service.

Greatness is found in serving. In taking the initiative to wash the grubby feet of His disciples, Jesus took upon Himself the lowliest task usually reserved for the most junior of servants. As we volunteer, initiate with kindness, surprise others with unexpected generosity, we demonstrate a greatness of character that God truly celebrates.

Greatness is expressed in humility. This is not self-deprecation or a willingness to be a doormat for others, but a settled sense that we will not allow pride or arrogance to taint our souls. We are open, teachable, and willing to allow those we love and trust to confront us about our failings.

Greatness is found in selflessness, where we live for the glory of God rather than to make ourselves look good. Herod wanted to be remembered as "great," building the Herodium just south of Jerusalem, a memorial to his own victories in battle.

Greatness creates a beautiful example and legacy. Herod's legacy was evil. After his death, his son Antipas served as tetrarch over Galilee (Matt. 14:1; Luke 3:1). He is the Herod most referred to in the Gospels, as he reigned during Jesus' years of ministry. Antipas probably inherited some of his father's shrewd ways, since Jesus referred to him as a "fox" (Luke 13:32). Herod Antipas is also mentioned at the trial of Jesus (Luke 23:6–12).

And what of that place that Herod built to honor himself, the Herodium? It would be his place of burial. He became very ill, apparently from arteriosclerosis, and he knew he was facing the grave—yet still he worried about his popularity, or lack of it. So worried was he that his death would not be mourned (a justifiable anxiety), he issued a command from his deathbed that leaders from all parts of Judea were to be locked inside the great hippodrome at Jericho. The plan was that when Herod died and his passing was announced, archers were to massacre these thousands of captives in cold blood. The hideous plan was that this mass killing would result in universal mourning associated with his death, even though the tears would not be for him. Although the leaders were gathered, the order was never given by Herod's son Archelaus and his sister Salome.

Herod was concerned about his legacy, but his plan that his death would make an impact was totally misguided and failed. We are all building a legacy, whatever our age and stage of life. What we do today will make an impact, and perhaps be remembered and celebrated, or pondered with sadness, in the future. But the baby whom Herod sought to kill grew, and became the teacher and miracle worker of Galilee and the Savior and Redeemer of Gethsemane and Golgotha. The earthly king of the Jews died with few, if any, mourners. The true King of the Jews, and King of Kings, is celebrated around the world today, not just as a historical figure, but also as the death-defeating freedom fighter. He is risen and walks into another year with us. In Him we put our trust.

If you are using the DVD, watch session 8.

STUDY AND DISCUSSION

1. What can we do when jealousy or envy strikes us?
2. What does being humble involve?
3. Consider: What's your greatest achievement in your life to date—the act or episode of which you are most proud (in the best sense of the word "proud")?

GOING DEEPER

Author Richard Rohr wrote, "Humility and honesty are really the same thing. A humble person is simply a brutally honest person about the whole truth. You and I came along a few years ago, and we're going to be gone in a few years. The only honest response to life is an honest one."[2] Discuss these thoughts.

THIS SESSION'S CHALLENGE

Is there an opportunity to serve that might involve hard work, lack of recognition, and appreciation (or both) that I need to embrace?

DAILY BIBLE NOTES: HEROD "THE GREAT"
Day 1. Herod: Ignored by Angels

Read: Luke 2:8–21; 1 Corinthians 1:26–31

Focus: "And there were shepherds living out in the fields nearby, keeping watch over their flocks at night. An angel of the Lord appeared to them, and the glory of the Lord shone around them, and they were terrified" (Luke 2:8–9).

It's interesting to see just who God spoke to about the most momentous event in human history since Creation itself—the incarnation of His Son, who came to rescue us all. We might have expected that kings, including Herod, would be informed of the coming of the King of Kings. A new kingdom, unlike any other reign, was being ushered in. But instead, the news comes to a teenaged virgin, her confused fiancé, and on this night, a gaggle of shepherds out on the night shift. Shepherding was officially listed as a "sinner trade" at that time. These agricultural workers were thought of as untrustworthy, often stealing sheep and allowing their flocks to graze on private land without permission.

But the despot with his palaces was ignored and, as we'll see, probably didn't get to hear about the birth of the Messiah until two years after it had happened.

Right from the start, the outsiders were brought in, and the insiders, who were used to occupying the halls of power and information, were clearly placed on the outside in what author Donald Kraybill calls "the upside-down kingdom" of Jesus.

Perhaps you don't feel very significant, and that your opinions and insights are not sought after. Broadly, you feel like an outsider all too often. But you are included among the people of God, to whom the good news has come. Be grateful today!

Pray: I'm grateful, Lord, that I have been one who has heard and responded to Your good news. Amen.

Day 2. Joseph Escaped Herod's Clutches

Read: Matthew 2:1–23; 2 Corinthians 12:10

Focus: "When they had gone, an angel of the Lord appeared to Joseph in a dream. 'Get up,' he said, 'take the child and his mother and escape to Egypt. Stay there until I tell you, for Herod is going to search for the child to kill him'" (Matt. 2:13).

We celebrate the truth that Jesus was born, our rescuer, our redeemer. And as we've been considering some of the rogues and rascals of the Bible, we celebrate the truth that even though we, too, are described in Scripture as being former "enemies" of God, lost, sinful, like sheep going astray. Now we have been saved by the wondrous work of Christ. In His coming, Jesus was dogged by those who opposed His work, but through the work of the Spirit, He triumphed over them all.

Joseph doesn't tend to get too much credit in the whole story, but I'd like us to celebrate him as an ordinary man who, with the help of God, was able to escape the threats and violence of Herod. Sensitive to the voice of God, he received repeated inspired dreams. An angel appeared to him during one of those dreams and gave revelation that steered Joseph away from his previous decision to respectfully end his relationship with Mary. And then another angelic appearance, again during a dream, warned Joseph of Herod's plans to seek out and kill the Messiah. Two further dreams led Joseph to settle his family in Nazareth, after returning from being fugitives in Egypt.

Salvation has come and is offered to all. And we affirm the truth that God works with ordinary, weak people (there's nothing else to choose from!), like Joseph, like you, and like me, to fulfill His kingdom purposes.

Pray: I am ordinary, and often weak, Lord, but You are extraordinary, and mighty, and Your Spirit dwells within me. Amen.

Day 3. Herod: Enemy of the Light

Read: Matthew 2:1–18; 5:14

Focus: "When Herod realized that he had been outwitted by the Magi, he was furious, and he gave orders to kill all the boys in Bethlehem and its vicinity who were two years old and under, in accordance with the time he had learned from the Magi" (Matt. 2:16).

It was during one of those prayer times that happen before a service. The little gaggle of leaders gathered in a circle and was sharing prayers and murmured "Amens" of agreement. Suddenly one of the group began to fervently intercede against the interference of the devil, loudly binding any satanic activity that might hinder the effectiveness of the service that was about to start. I looked up and glanced across the room to see a fellow leader staring back at me, rolling his eyes, an expression of "this is a bit over the top, isn't it?" on his face. I understood his look. Some Christians are over-preoccupied with the enemy. But the other extreme, where we forget that we are involved in a spiritual battle, is equally dangerous. We are people of the light, and there are powers of darkness that seek to resist what we do in Jesus' name.

Herod was not just a killer, although he was consistently murderous, as we'll see in tomorrow's Bible notes; he was also a sworn enemy of the light. The Talmud relates a story where, after killing many rabbis, he was told by a blind rabbi, Bava ben Buta, that he had "snuffed out the light of the world"—the common description for rabbis in Jesus' day.

Whether or not he knew it, Herod's campaign of infanticide in Nazareth was another attempt to extinguish the true light of the world, Christ. And Jesus says that we, His people, are the light of the world now. Light always beats darkness. We don't need to fear, but we shouldn't be oblivious to the reality of spiritual warfare either.

Pray: Help me to be aware of the battle, and help me to stand strong in Your authority, mighty God. Amen.

Day 4. Herod: Heartless and Hard Hearted

Read: Matthew 2:1–18; Hebrews 3:12–15

Focus: "When Herod realized that he had been outwitted by the Magi, he was furious, and he gave orders to kill all the boys in Bethlehem and its vicinity who were two years old and under, in accordance with the time he had learned from the Magi" (Matt. 2:16).

Sin begets sin. When we harden our hearts and stifle our consciences, we tread a downhill path, on which we gradually become impervious to pangs of guilt about what we are doing. Herod is an extreme example of this pattern. The infanticide at Nazareth, which most likely resulted in about seven deaths of small children, was not an isolated incident. We already have seen that when Herod shaped the Temple in Jerusalem, he had a large Roman eagle placed in the entryway. A group of pious Jews vandalized the emblem, seeing that it represented idolatry and oppression. Herod had them arrested, dragged in chains to his residence in Jericho, and burned alive.

Herod was somewhat unlucky in love, to say the least. He had ten wives but loved his favorite, Mariamne, who hated him with equal passion, because he had killed her brother, Aristobulus. Twice he ordered that she be killed if he failed to return from a critical mission. He finally killed her anyway, as well as her grandfather, her mother, his brother-in-law, and three of his sons, not to mention numerous subjects. In his advancing paranoia, he was continually writing to Rome for permission to execute one or two of his sons for treason. Finally even his patron and friend Augustus had to admit, "I'd rather be Herod's pig than his son." It was not only a play on the similar-sounding Greek words for *son* and *pig*, but a wry reference to the fact that pork, at least, was not consumed by Jews.

Are we headed on a downhill path?

Pray: Speak to me, Lord, when temptation whispers. Amen.

Day 5. Insecurity

Read: Matthew 2:1–3; James 3:13–14

Focus: "When King Herod heard this he was disturbed, and all Jerusalem with him" (Matt. 2:3).

Insecurity. Often it's not a lingering issue quietly dwelling just under our skin, but a driving force that compels us to keep up, to outshine, to compete, and even to discredit those whom we view as competitors. It seems that Herod was a horrendously insecure soul, despite all his wealth and power. Even a baby tagged as "King of the Jews" threatened him, the Roman-appointed king of the Jews. Insecurity drove him to kill his brother-in-law Aristobulus, who was becoming a favorite with the masses. Couple this with his compulsive problem with jealousy, and you have a man who has to build bigger and better in order to endlessly prove himself.

Once again, he is an extreme example, but we must ask ourselves: Are we secure in our own skin, with the gifts we have, with our role in life? We're constantly drip-fed the lie that we need to look a particular way in order to fit in. But even though the marketing voices are loud and insistent, they sell a lie. Insecurity is a negative fuel.

Pray: May my perception of myself be rooted in Your love, care, and purposes for my life, rather than the superficial markers created by our culture. Amen.

Day 6. Herod: State-Tainted Religion

Read: Matthew 10:1–20; 5:13–16

Herod's temple in Jerusalem was a spectacular sight, a true wonder to behold.

Desperate to curry favor from his own people, and wanting to make amends for his cruel persecution of some members of the rabbinic community, Herod set about to rebuild the Temple. It took ten thousand men ten years just to build the retaining walls. It was part of a five-hundred-meter-long plateau that could house twenty-four football fields, a gathering place for the six to seven million Jews who lived in the Roman Empire and who would make regular pilgrimages to Jerusalem to attend the various feasts and festivals. But the Jews hated the huge Roman eagle Herod had placed in the main entrance.

Herod wanted to be popular religiously and politically, but faith and politics don't always mix well. Being a good Christian is not the same as being a compliant citizen: sometimes we have to make a stand against the popular view rather than go with the flow.

Ponder: Can you think of an example of where church and state might come into conflict?

THE MOB IN THESSALONICA

The Call to Faithfulness in the War

CONNECTING WITH ONE ANOTHER

Fashion is dictated by a few, but followed by the crowd. What are some of the more outrageous fashion choices that you have made in the past?

KEY THOUGHT THIS SESSION

Opposition is part of the Christian life, and it will come as we part company with the consensus view of the majority. We're called to be faithful when we face difficulties because we march to the different drumbeat of the kingdom.

SCRIPTURE TO READ

Acts 17:1–9

When Paul and his companions had passed through Amphipolis and Apollonia, they came to Thessalonica, where there was a Jewish synagogue. As was his custom, Paul went into the synagogue, and on three Sabbath days he reasoned with them from the Scriptures, explaining and proving that the Messiah had to suffer and rise from the dead. "This Jesus I am proclaiming to you is the Messiah," he said. Some of the Jews were persuaded and joined Paul and Silas, as did a large number of God-fearing Greeks and quite a few prominent women.

But other Jews were jealous; so they rounded up some bad characters from the marketplace, formed a mob and started a riot in the city. They rushed to Jason's house in search of Paul and Silas in order to bring them out to the crowd. But when they did not find them, they dragged Jason and some other believers before the city officials, shouting: "These men who have caused trouble all over the world have now come here, and Jason has welcomed them into his house. They are all defying Caesar's decrees, saying that there is another king, one called Jesus." When they heard this, the crowd and the city officials were thrown into turmoil. Then they made Jason and the others post bond and let them go.

1 Thessalonians 2:1–2

You know, brothers and sisters, that our visit to you was not without results. We had previously suffered and been treated outrageously in Philippi, as you know, but with the help of our God we dared to tell you his gospel in the face of strong opposition.

1 Thessalonians 2:18

For we wanted to come to you—certainly I, Paul, did, again and again—but Satan blocked our way.

2 Corinthians 11:23–28

I have worked much harder, been in prison more frequently, been flogged more severely, and been exposed to death again and again. Five times I received from the Jews the forty lashes minus one. Three times I was beaten with rods, once I was pelted with stones, three times I was shipwrecked, I spent a night and a day in the open sea, I have been constantly on the move. I have been in danger from rivers, in danger from bandits, in danger from my fellow Jews, in danger from Gentiles; in danger in the city, in danger in the

country, in danger at sea; and in danger from false
believers. I have labored and toiled and have often
gone without sleep; I have known hunger and thirst
and have often gone without food; I have been cold
and naked. Besides everything else, I face daily the
pressure of my concern for all the churches.

FOR YOUR CONSIDERATION

An angry crowd is a frightening sight—and a rioting crowd is dangerous. Spurring one another on, finding courage from being part of
the group, a mob can cause untold damage to people and property.
And so we turn now, not to an individual rogue, but rather to a
group of zealots who opposed the gospel in the city of Thessalonica.

Paul and Silas arrived in the city having faced false accusations
(and a night in prison) in Philippi. Severely beaten and held in stocks
there, they had been liberated from jail by a God-sent earthquake.
Undeterred, they continue their missionary trek, only to meet yet
more opposition in Thessalonica. Their message was thought radical
in a seaport with a reputation for immorality:

> Thessalonica is the first seaport reached by the
> gospel. Seaports were places of prosperity and licen-
> tiousness. Wherever men arrive from the sea there
> are red light districts to meet their needs.[1]

Before we look at the rogues in this episode more carefully, let's
realize that God's direct and obvious intervention in one situation

doesn't mean that He will do the same in another. No earthquake caused the ground to shake when some of the Thessalonian believers were hauled in front of civic officials and falsely accused, which must have been a terrifying experience.

We often view unanswered prayer as an obstacle to faith, but answered prayer creates questions too: Why was this person apparently healed, and that suffering soul died a painful death with no physical healing evident? The "helpful earthquake" doesn't always arrive.

Trust is always needed in the walk of faith, because those questions are not easily answered. What is true always is that God is with us. His ways and works vary, but the promise of His presence and help is totally consistent.

Considering the mob, pastor Kent Hughes wrote:

> Some of the Jews rejected Paul and, having become inflamed with a misplaced zeal, went to the center of town and recruited a mob. Our text calls them "wicked men" (NASB), and the King James Version says, "lewd fellows of the baser sort." I like A. T. Robertson's rendering—"bums."[2]

As believers, we are called to be nonconformists because of this simple fact: the crowd might be powerful, loud, insistent, but the crowd can be wrong, as author John Stott argued:

> On the one hand, as Christian people, we are called to be conscientious and law-abiding citizens, not revolutionaries. On the other hand, the kingship of

Jesus has unavoidable political implications since,
as his loyal subjects, we must refuse to give to any
ruler or ideology the supreme homage and total
obedience which are due to him alone.[3]

In refusing to yield to the consensus, it's not that we want to disagree
for the sake of disagreement. Rather, we are aligning ourselves with the
great purposes of God for His planet and for all people everywhere. We
are people who want to see the world turned "the right way up."

"These people who have been turning the world upside down,"
they said, "have come here." Well, yes. Paul would probably, if
pushed, say that they were turning the world the right way up,
because it was currently upside down, and he would most likely have
been quite pleased to see that people had at least understood that he
wasn't just offering them a new religious experience, but announcing
to the world that its creator was at last setting it all right.[4]

It was illegal to try to evangelize a Roman citizen. But Paul and
his team were accountable to a higher authority. And so are we.

This episode also shows us that we need wisdom for everyday
life, because our responses to the changing circumstances that we
experience will differ.

In the city visited prior to Thessalonica, Philippi, Paul and Silas
had been badly treated and falsely accused by the city officials. When
asked to leave the city, they stood their ground and claimed their
rights as Roman citizens:

But Paul said to the officers: "They beat us publicly
without a trial, even though we are Roman citizens,

and threw us into prison. And now do they want to get rid of us quietly? No! Let them come themselves and escort us out."

The officers reported this to the magistrates, and when they heard that Paul and Silas were Roman citizens, they were alarmed. They came to appease them and escorted them from the prison, requesting them to leave the city. After Paul and Silas came out of the prison, they went to Lydia's house, where they met with the brothers and sisters and encouraged them. Then they left. (Acts 16:37–40)

In Thessalonica, Paul and Silas were not imprisoned or beaten, but Jason, a man who had offered them hospitality in his home, was arrested and ordered to post bond. However, Paul made no fuss or complaint, perhaps to protect Jason and the new believers in the city from further harm. He and his team quietly left for Berea, where they and their message would receive a much more favorable response.

Now the Berean Jews were of more noble character than those in Thessalonica, for they received the message with great eagerness and examined the Scriptures every day to see if what Paul said was true. (Acts 17:11)

Navigating life with the same wooden responses won't work: every day brings fresh challenges, and we need to seek God's direction and wisdom as life unfolds.

Finally, once again we see the reality of spiritual warfare in the riot-ous Thessalonians. Earlier we saw that, in the life of Judas Iscariot, Satan was at work behind the scenes, so Paul recognized the work of the enemy behind the angry eyes and screaming voices of the Thessalonian mob. The battle was ongoing, and not limited to this one event. Repeatedly Paul wanted to return to the city but said that "Satan blocked our way."

The word Paul used is a term that comes from the military. In order to stop the advance of enemy armies, soldiers would tear up and destroy the road to hinder their passage. Warfare imagery is embedded in the metaphor; Satan himself being their adversary. The battle was over the souls of the Thessalonian believers whom Satan tempted to commit the sin of apostasy. One of his tactics was to bar the way so the apostles could not return to the church. Despite the opposition, they did manage to send Timothy back (1 Thess. 3:1–2), and the church itself continued on in faith and love (3:5–6). Sometime later Paul was able to return to Macedonia and Thessalonica (Acts 19:21–22; 20:1–6; 1 Cor. 16:5; 2 Cor. 1:16; 2:13; 7:5; 1 Tim. 1:3). God had responded to their fervent prayers (1 Thess. 3:10–11). In this spiritual warfare, Satan is hardly an omnipotent adversary. But he is a real adversary.[5]

As we end this study, we realize that we, too, are involved in warfare. Christ has won victory over the powers of darkness at the cross, but in the meantime we have to stand strong, firm, and faithful until the final day of His coming, when the battle will be finally and completely over.

Perhaps those who went rogue were oblivious, or ignored the reality of that war, and so made choices that led them away from God's purposes. May we learn from their mistakes and live boldly for and with God, all the way until that great final day of His appearing.

If you are using the DVD, watch session 9.

STUDY AND DISCUSSION

1. In his writings, Paul doesn't insist that every obstacle he encountered came as a result of Satan's work. But he is very aware that there is an enemy who opposes God's work. How can we maintain a balanced attitude toward spiritual warfare?

2. "Answered prayer creates questions"—consider the ways you have experienced this.

3. "Navigating life with the same wooden responses won't work: every day brings fresh challenges, and we need to seek God's direction and wisdom as life unfolds." Can you share an episode from your life where you have found that to be true?

GOING DEEPER

"The crowd can be wrong." Where are some of the areas we as Christians might need to break stride with our culture?

DAILY BIBLE NOTES: THE MOB IN THESSALONICA
Day 1. God at Work, but So Is the Devil

Read: Acts 17:1–4; 1 Thessalonians 2:17–20

A headline caught my attention today. The BBC, reporting a story of terrible abuse that was perpetuated in the name of religion (Christian religion, actually), cited "belief in the existence of Satan" as a reason for the atrocity. That's a dangerous generalization, because the Bible clearly describes a figure called Satan, and as followers of Christ, we acknowledge that there is a personal power of evil in the world today. But the headline made talk about Satan seem quaint, outdated, and ridiculous. And then there are some Christians who are so fixated with blaming every incidental bad thing that happens in life on the devil. In their obsession with him, they make the very idea of his existence seem ridiculous.

God was clearly very much on the move in Thessalonica with key influencers in the city coming to Christ. But as God acts, so the enemy counteracts. Paul would later write about how he wanted to spend time with the Thessalonian Christians, "but Satan blocked our way" (1 Thess. 2:18). We saw earlier, when we looked at the life of Herod, that there is a personal power of evil in the world to be reckoned with. It's worth repeating here, because we'd better believe it.

Ponder: Do you tend to ignore the existence of personal evil or veer toward excessive preoccupation with the devil?

Day 2. Misguided Passion

Read: Acts 17:1–5; 18:1–13

Focus: "But other Jews were jealous" (Acts 17:5).

It's a subject that Christians don't talk about much: Christian fanaticism. We see faith as a matter of all-in commitment, of complete surrender to the purposes of God. So why would we want to consider fanaticism as being a potential threat? Besides, it's been said that one definition of a fanatic is someone who is more committed to Jesus than we are. While that's a catchy little saying, it doesn't acknowledge the truth that it's possible to become an extremist even in our Christian faith. And I'm not just talking about the historical excesses of the Crusades, or the madness of the so-called Westboro Baptist Church, whose members trek across America yelling at gay people and even picketing the funerals of those who have died in military service. I've met Christians who are so zealous that they hold extreme views and rant at others who dare to disagree with them, insisting that they alone are the guardians of true orthodoxy.

As we read that some Jews were jealous, we might jump to the conclusion that they were envious of Paul's influence in their city. But Paul also used the word "jealous" elsewhere to describe his own zealous behavior before he became a Christian. So eager was he for the purity of Judaism that he relentlessly pursued the followers of Jesus. It's possible that Paul's opponents, like some others in Corinth (Acts 18:13), were concerned that he was liberalizing their Jewish faith. They were driven by misguided passion.

Let's be all in for Jesus, but not over the top.

Pray: Father, I want to be neither insipid nor excessive in my faith. Please show me the right way. Amen.

Day 3. Blind Spots

Read: Acts 17:1–5; Luke 6:1–11

Focus: "But other Jews were jealous; so they rounded up some bad characters from the marketplace, formed a mob and started a riot in the city" (Acts 17:5).

We call it a blind spot. Driving on a busy road, you glance in the side mirror to check to see if you can safely overtake, and all looks clear. But there's a second or two when a car doesn't appear in your mirror, and if you don't double-check, disaster could result.

We can have blind spots about ourselves too. I've noticed this as a result of being on the planet for six decades. It's the ability to point the finger of criticism at others, while all the time ignoring (or being oblivious to) the glaring reality that I, too, am guilty of the very attitude that I'm critical of. Jesus put it more simply: we can go searching for specks in the eyes of others, while ignoring the plank of wood in our own eyes.

Perhaps that's what happened as these fervent Jews rounded up a band of rabble-rousers, who were hanging around (one translator calls them "loafers") in the marketplace, and urged them to attack the Christian community. They insisted that the believers were troublemakers, even as they themselves deliberately made trouble by inciting a riot! Perhaps this was just rank hypocrisy—or maybe they just didn't see the rather obvious contradiction.

Perhaps you're in a situation where you are so focused on the failings of someone else that you don't see the very same failing in your own life. We can all be guilty of it. Let's pray that God will help us to see what we don't currently see, lest we end up being carping hypocrites, experts in the minute faults of others, oblivious to the greater fault in ourselves.

Pray: How keenly I can see the faults of others, Lord. And how blind I can be to my own. Grant me a heart of grace and mercy. Amen.

Day 4. A Subversive Message

Read: Acts 17:6–7; Matthew 5:13–16

Focus: "But when they did not find them, they dragged Jason and some other believers before the city officials" (Acts 17:6).

When people are angry, they look for someone to vent their rage on—and if the one who angered them is not around, somebody else is likely to get the blame. That's exactly what happened here, as the angry crowd headed to the house where Paul and Silas were staying. Unable to find them, they attacked a man called Jason, the owner of that home, and hauled him and some of his fellow Christians before the "politarchs"—citizens who oversaw the first steps of legal proceedings.

The charges were very serious, amounting to treason. The worship of idols was woven into every part of Roman life; temples were community centers and banking halls. Senate meetings opened with sacrifices; battles began and ended with prayers. And the emperor was the primary priest of the entire Roman cult. Anything that displeased the "gods" could lead to disaster: economic failure, fire, famine—people believed that these could come upon a community if the gods were not respected locally. Now, these Christians were declaring that there was only one true King, Jesus. The gospel was a threat to the traditional values of the culture.

To be a Christian is to follow a kingdom agenda that will invariably clash with the accepted values of those around us. We are called to be distinctive and different, people who live lives that stand out like a beacon on a hill, with the saltiness that flavors food. At times, that might make people angry. But that's the pathway we're called to walk.

Pray: Grant me boldness to make a stand for You when it is called for, Father. Amen.

Day 5. Paul's Response

Read: Acts 17:1–10; 16:16–40

Focus: "As soon as it was night, the believers sent Paul and Silas away to Berea" (Acts 17:10).

Perhaps you've met them. Ruffled by every incident they view as unjust, quickly offended by any stray word they might have overheard, they insist on holding endless meetings to straighten out every issue. These people can create havoc in church life, because they seem delighted when there is a disagreement to resolve. And they don't usually do too well in friendship and marriage, because they are apparently incapable of being magnanimous and content with just moving forward when they are irritated: everything needs explanation, clarification, and quite often, heartfelt apology.

Paul and his team experienced multiple episodes of false accusation, corruption, and injustice, and sometimes this cost him dearly, suffering beatings and imprisonment as well as thwarting his missional plans. There were times when he stood his ground and demanded apology and appeasement, because as a Roman citizen, he had clear legal rights, and he used that status to confront those who treated him badly. We see this following his incarceration in Philippi. But compare that with his response to the rioting mob (and the city officials) in Thessalonica; perhaps more concerned about the welfare of Jason and the other believers in the city, Paul quietly moved on and headed out of town, unwilling to pursue the matter further. Not everything needs sorting out. Know when to stand up for what is right—and when to shrug your shoulders and move on. If we fail to know the difference, we'll end up fighting battles that need not be fought.

Pray: Lord, help me to respond to the unfolding challenges that come in life, to know the best way for each different situation. Amen.

Day 6. Finishing Well

Read: 2 Timothy 4:6–8; 1 Corinthians 9:24–27

Focus: "I have fought the good fight, I have finished the race, I have kept the faith" (2 Tim. 4:7).

Our journey, looking at some of the rogues and scoundrels of the Bible, is finished. Over the last nine sessions, we've considered some of the men and women of history who made poor choices; their names are forever associated with sin and failure. All, with the wonderful exception of Saul who became the apostle Paul, continued their downhill trajectories.

Today, I want to end our reflections by returning one last time to Saul/Paul, the man who was so unlikely to become such a dynamic Christian leader, but the one who accomplished so much. Saul didn't just have a momentary encounter on the Damascus Road; rather, this was a turning point that changed him forever. As he faced the end of his life, he knew that, whatever the trials of being under house arrest and the threat of execution, he had completed his task and purpose on the earth. Now, he was ready and willing to depart and be with Christ.

In the Christian family, we are all living different stories. Some of us are flourishing, some really struggling. The journey of life will never be without its challenges. But whatever the emotional and circumstantial weather, may each of us follow Paul's example, rather than the negative examples of those who went rogue, because this much is true: God is love, God is faithful, and His way is the very best way for each and every one of us.

Pray: By Your grace, Father, may I walk all the days of my life with You. Amen.

NOTES

SESSION 1: CAIN

1. R. Kent Hughes, *Hebrews: An Anchor for the Soul*, vol. 2 (Wheaton, IL: Crossway Books, 1993), 68.

2. Hughes, *Hebrews*, 69.

3. Henrik Ibsen, *Brand* (play, 1867).

SESSION 2: THE ELDER BROTHER

1. Ibn al-Tayyib (AD 1043), Tafsir II, 186.

2. Catherine Mowry LaCugna, *God for Us: The Trinity and the Christian Life* (San Francisco: HarperCollins, 1991), 401.

SESSION 3: POTIPHAR'S WIFE

1. Andrew J. Schmutzer, "Digging Deeper. Learning Character over Comfort: The Purification of Temptation" (unpublished paper, 2003), 2.

SESSION 4: SAUL THE PERSECUTOR

1. Brennan Manning, *Ruthless Trust: The Ragamuffin's Path to God* (San Francisco: HarperSanFrancisco, 2000), 115.

2. Michael Griffiths, *Cinderella with Amnesia: A Restatement in Contemporary Terms of the Biblical Doctrine of the Church* (Nottingham, UK: InterVarsity, 1975), 23.

3. This famous saying is often attributed to Sigmund Freud, though no definite source is available at the time of this printing. Research implies the quote is taken from writings concerning Freudian view.

4. For information on this saying, read "Who Wrote 'Risk'? Is the Mystery Solved?," *The Anais Nin Blog*, March 5, 2013, http://anaisninblog.skybluepress.com /2013/03/who-wrote-risk-is-the-mystery-solved/.

SESSION 5: MICHAL, DAUGHTER OF KING SAUL

1. Bill T. Arnold, *The NIV Application Commentary: 1 & 2 Samuel* (Grand Rapids, MI: Zondervan, 2003), 460.

2. Gnana Robinson, *Let Us Be Like the Nations: A Commentary on the Books of 1 and 2 Samuel* (Grand Rapids, MI: Eerdmans, 1993), 184.

3. Philip Yancey, *What's So Amazing about Grace?* (Grand Rapids, MI: Zondervan, 1997).

4. Gabriel García Márquez, *Love in the Time of Cholera*, trans. Edith Grossman (New York: Penguin, 1989).

5. François Mauriac, *The Knot of Vipers*, trans. G. Hopkins (New York: Penguin, 1985).

6. Charles Finney, *Revival Lectures*, cited in David Mains, *The Sense of His Presence* (Waco, TX: Word Books, 1988), 69–70.

SESSION 6: JEZEBEL

1. J. R. Miller, *The Every Day of Life* (New York: Thomas Y. Crowell, 1892), 246–47.

2. Janet Howe Gaines, "How Bad Was Jezebel?," *Bible Review*, October 2000.

SESSION 8: HEROD "THE GREAT"

1. Josephus, *The Jewish War*, 1.27.6.

2. Richard Rohr, *Everything Goes* (New York: Crossroad, 1999), 103.

SESSION 9: THE MOB IN THESSALONICA

1. David Cook, *Teaching Acts: Unlocking the Book of Acts for the Bible Teacher*, ed. D. Jackman and R. Sydserff (Ross-shire, UK: Proclamation Trust Media, 2007), 226–27.

2. R. Kent Hughes, *Acts: The Church Afire* (Wheaton, IL: Crossway Books, 1996), 224.

3. John R. W. Stott, *The Message of Acts: The Spirit, the Church and the World* (Leicester, UK: InterVarsity, 1994), 273.

4. N. T. Wright, *Acts for Everyone, Part 2: Chapters 13–28* (London: Society for Promoting Christian Knowledge, 2008), 78.

5. Gene L. Green, *The Letters to the Thessalonians* (Grand Rapids, MI: W. B. Eerdmans, 2002), 152.